PRAISE FOR
CULTURE IS EVERYTHING

"Peter Drucker taught us that culture eats strategy for breakfast. But how do you build a strong, sustainable company culture? With a repeatable system and checklist. Tristan White's Culture Is Everything System makes the complex task of building a strong culture much simpler by design. If you are an entrepreneur or leader and want to build a strong culture, then read this book for a practical case study in how it's accomplished.

> **—VERNE HARNISH,** author of *Scaling Up (Rockefeller Habits 2.0)*

"Tristan knows better than anyone the impact of culture on a company. We worked together years ago, and his results have proven that his insights are worth reading by any company that wants to grow. I've loved watching his year-over-year trajectory to becoming the number-one company to work for."

> **—CAMERON HEROLD,** author of *Double Double* and *Meetings Suck*

"From start-up to Australia's best place to work, Tristan recognised his competitive advantage would come from attracting and retaining the best people. This book shows you how he did it."

> **—GLEN CARLSON,** cofounder and managing director, Dent Global

"Great entrepreneurs walk their walk and talk their talk. They wholeheartedly believe that business should be used as a force for good and feel a deep level of personal responsibility to make sure theirs is. Tristan White knows better than anyone that your people and your culture are the ones to drive this mission, and he's devoted his life to ensuring his company means more than a pay cheque to everyone involved. I've long respected Tristan for his values and ethics and am excited to see what impact he makes by sharing his learnings with the world. Go Tristan!"

—**EMMA ISAACS,** founder / global CEO, Business Chicks

"It takes a relentless commitment to improving the lives of others to have achieved such accolades as a best employer. Tristan has a clear sense of vision, he knows why he does what he does, and he is happy to share with those who want to learn and see what is possible when you 'give a damn' for other human beings. This is a wonderful story that will inspire you to greatness. #smallbizsuccess"

—**NAOMI SIMSON,** entrepreneur, NaomiSimson.com

"Ninety percent of the 332 successful small business owners I've interviewed cite 'happy staff' as a critical success factor. Tristan's unwavering passion for creating a workplace that ensures such happiness is palpable. Having worked in a corporate cubicle for twenty-two years, I wish my past employers had the opportunity to have read this book."

—**TIM REID,** host of *The Small Business Big Marketing Show*

"Tristan's journey has so many lessons across all walks of life—both personal and professional. His story and that of The Physio Co. is an inspiring one and a demonstration of how passion, tenacity, and laser-beam focus can help you achieve your goals. I see our members challenged every day with the rapidly changing health and well-being landscape. They all share a commitment to improve the life of Australians via physiotherapy. Tristan is living proof of this ethos. In a world of digital disruption, it is refreshing to see a relationship-/people-based approach creating a successful business. Tristan has paved the way for the 'social-physiotherapist' of the future. This book is a powerful read."

—**CRIS MASSIS,** CEO, Australian Physiotherapy Association

"In Culture Is Everything *Tristan White provides the proven formula: a repeatable system, directed towards a clear vision and a foundation of core values—all supported by recognition and repeatable with ongoing storytelling. Tristan now facilitates all entrepreneurs to do the same with his Culture is Everything Checklist used at The Physio Co. Now put this book and provided checklist into play in your organization!"*

—**JACK DALY,** three-time Amazon bestselling author, www.jackdaly.net

"Businesses with strong, aligned cultures outperform other businesses every day of the week. My business, The Entourage, is committed to building a phenomenal culture, and we've won awards for it. Tristan's Culture Is Everything System is a practical, easy-to-follow approach to help leaders, entrepreneurs, and business owners understand how to create a world-class culture for their team."

—**JACK DELOSA,** founder and CEO, The Entourage.

"There is no doubt that a foundation pillar to a great workplace is a great culture. And culture has to be created in joint partnership with enthusiastic people who have clear direction and a common goal.

For the first ten years in business, I was the only employee, and when I started building the Carman's team, I didn't have a clear plan on how to build a company culture. I just started doing little things that I thought would make a difference to create an environment where people loved coming to work.

If only I'd had a system to fast track this process! In Culture Is Everything, Tristan has captured his way to create a strong and systemised culture. It's a great book that provides an insight of what it takes to build a great place to work."

—**CAROLYN CRESWELL,** founder & managing director, Carman's Fine Foods

"Building a great business takes time, takes strong leadership, and takes a commitment to creating a robust culture. Greencross grew from a small group of veterinary practices to a large, ASX-listed healthcare success story based upon a people-focused culture. If you want to learn the foundations of strong growth centred on a robust culture, read Tristan's book and follow his lead."

—GLEN RICHARDS, founder and former CEO, Greencross Limited (ASX: GXL)

CULTURE

IS EVERYTHING

THE STORY AND SYSTEM OF A
START-UP THAT BECAME

AUSTRALIA'S
BEST PLACE TO WORK

CULTURE

IS EVERYTHING

TRISTAN WHITE

Advantage®

Published by Advantage, Charleston, South Carolina.
Member of Advantage Media Group.

ADVANTAGE is a registered trademark, and the Advantage colophon is a trademark of Advantage Media Group, Inc.

Printed in the United States of America.

10 9 8 7 6 5 4 3 2 1

ISBN: 978-1-59932-663-4
LCCN: 2017932465

Cover design by Katie Biondo.

This publication is designed to provide accurate and authoritative information in regard to the subject matter covered. It is sold with the understanding that the publisher is not engaged in rendering legal, accounting, or other professional services. If legal advice or other expert assistance is required, the services of a competent professional person should be sought.

Advantage Media Group is proud to be a part of the Tree Neutral® program. Tree Neutral offsets the number of trees consumed in the production and printing of this book by taking proactive steps such as planting trees in direct proportion to the number of trees used to print books. To learn more about Tree Neutral, please visit **www.treeneutral.com.**

Advantage Media Group is a publisher of business, self-improvement, and professional development books. We help entrepreneurs, business leaders, and professionals share their Stories, Passion, and Knowledge to help others Learn & Grow. Do you have a manuscript or book idea that you would like us to consider for publishing? Please visit **advantagefamily.com** or call **1.866.775.1696.**

To past, present and future members of The Physio Co family (TPCers): thanks for inspiring me to learn, grow and improve every day.

CONTENTS

SECRET #3: EXECUTE RELENTLESSLY

SECRET #4: SHOW MORE LOVE

WHAT IT TAKES

THE CRITERIA TO BECOME A GREAT PLACE TO WORK

GREAT PLACE TO WORK CRITERIA

Australia's 50 Best Places to Work is an annual study and ranking by the Great Place to Work® Institute. The award is based on Great Place to Work input gathered on two assessment tools: the Trust Index© Employee Survey and the Culture Audit© Management Questionnaire.

The results of these surveys are used to determine rankings. The employee survey—which counts as two-thirds of the score—measures behaviours identified by the institute as creating a trusting workplace, the defining principle of a great workplace according to the institution. The culture audit gives human-resources personnel a chance to describe the company's unique culture.

The Great Place to Work® Institute has established standards that define a great workplace based on research data collected from more than ten million employees worldwide in companies of varying sizes, ages, industries and structures.

The findings are published annually in media channels such as *BRW* and *Australian Financial Review*, Australia's premiere business publications.

ACKNOWLEDGMENTS

WHEN I FOUNDED THE PHYSIO CO (TPC) in 2004 I was a twenty-four-year-old recently graduated physiotherapist with a dream of landing a job that inspired me. I never did find that job, so I've ended up creating it. In those early years, it was my parents, Marj and Roy, who really guided and supported me. Since then, along with the continued support of my Mum, it has been my wife, Kimberley, who has become my biggest fan and supporter. Another very important mentor, advisor and friend throughout my entire TPC journey has been Ben Hosking. I'm so very grateful to these caring people for the belief they have in me and the patience they have shown as I learn to be the best person I can be.

INTRO

AND GETTING TO KNOW ME
(TRISTAN)

G'DAY! THANKS SO MUCH for grabbing a copy of my book. I'm rapt that you're here with me and interested in building a great place to work. The world needs more great teams, organisations and workplaces.

My name's Tristan White, and over the last decade or so I have become the *Culture Is Everything* guy. That's the name of the blog that documents my journey as the founder and CEO of The Physio Co and the place where this *Culture Is Everything* journey first started. You can find that blog over at tristanwhite.com.au.

Culture Is Everything is the message that I now share with the audience at every speaking engagement I present, and that's the title of this book. *Culture Is Everything* is my approach to building a truly great business.

This book will help you understand that approach in more detail, but as an overview, *Culture Is Everything* is the method that I've created from

- thirteen years as a growth and culture-obsessed entrepreneur;

- attending conferences and learning events in Australia, USA, Canada, the Philippines, Greece and China;

- completing a master of business (MBA) degree at QUT;

- completing the Entrepreneurial Masters Program at MIT;

- reading mountains of books and articles (at least 250 business books!);

- learning from countless experiments and mistakes;

- working through challenges over months of accumulated sleepless nights;

- creating a high-performing hundred-plus-person team with an award-winning culture (from one person with an idea thirteen years earlier); and

- that team being ranked as one of Australia's 50 Best Places to Work for eight consecutive years and becoming Australia's Best Place to Work.

In short, my *Culture Is Everything* System is the outcome of years of learning, trying new things, making mistakes and refining an approach that has guided The Physio Co to more than thirteen years of continuous and profitable growth.

To me, creating a great place to work by building an aligned team that grows fast, celebrates often and genuinely cares for its people not only seems like the right thing to do, but over the long term—it works.

This book, however, is not a textbook. It's an experience-share based on the journey that I'm on. If you learn something that works for you, apply it. If what works at TPC doesn't resonate with you, don't use it. That's your choice. Please keep in mind, though, that the

Culture Is Everything System is not only for care-focussed organisations like the business that I lead. The same approach, using language tailored for your specific team/business/industry, is a repeatable system that has worked in fast-paced sales environments, in the construction industry, and even for a large team of garbage collectors. Whether your team has one, ten, a hundred, or a thousand team members, this method can work. The *Culture Is Everything* System has helped TPC scale from one person to a team of hundred-plus. The system is repeatable in small to medium-sized businesses and in one hundred to many thousand-person teams as well.

CULTURE WILL SAVE YOU AND YOUR BUSINESS

Lack of time is the biggest problem facing most business owners and senior leaders. Why? Because their team seems to need their constant attention, on both small and big challenges.

I was exactly the same, but I found a solution. Creating a strong culture changed my life in many ways.[1] *Culture Is Everything* means a culture by design (as opposed to a culture that occurs by default because no one is paying any attention to it).

As the founder of a small business, I survived the early years by relying on my curiosity and drive to even stay in business. I had belief in myself and my work.

But I wasn't always paying attention to culture.

In those early days, when we had a small team of fewer than fifteen people, my ambition and naivety caused problems that left me having next to no time in my life to do anything but work. At the

---

1   Tristan White, "How a Strong Culture Creates Time in Your Day," Dynamic Business, February 13, 2012, http://www.dynamicbusiness.com.au/small-business-resources/managing/how-a-strong-culture-creates-time-in-your-day-13022012.html.

same time, TPC was barely making enough money to pay me a wage. That wasn't the way it's supposed to be.

Fast-forward to today and we find TPC with an amazingly talented group of over a hundred team members located in more than 140 locations who together deliver more than two hundred thousand unique and memorable physiotherapy consultations to Australian seniors every year. There are also some huge differences in my working life: The Physio Co is five times the size, it is more profitable, I have my life back—and it no longer revolves around me working six to seven days a week!

What made the difference? If you said 'culture', then you already know.

Building a team based on the *Culture Is Everything* System has helped create hours in my day and has literally changed my life. It's not a quick fix, but it is one of the most sustainable and rewarding ways to simplify and grow a business.

UNDERSTANDING WHAT MAKES ME TICK

Before we dive into The Physio Co story and the systems you can use to build a strong culture, I'd like you to get to know me and my thoughts about work. Even before I became the *Culture Is Everything* guy, I wanted to find a job surrounded by people who inspired me to do great work. What eventually became the *Culture Is Everything* System has changed in small ways over the years, but the foundational ideas that influenced it remain the same.

The ideas that influence my approach are what I call the **Five Beliefs of Meaningful Work.**

1. I believe we spend so much time working that we have to find a way to enjoy it.

2. I believe we enjoy work when we're doing something useful for others.

3. I believe we enjoy work when we feel proud of doing the right thing in challenging situations.

4. I believe we enjoy work when there are defined boundaries around what we should be doing and we have some freedom around how to do it.

5. I believe every team, business and organisation can create this 'freedom within boundaries' environment that is the foundation of a strong culture.

There's plenty of research that has found that on their deathbed, people often regret having spent so much of their lives at work. I understand that, but I'm willing to challenge the concept to find a way for us to better blend our work with other parts of our life, so that we see our work among the best things we do—to blend work and life instead of trying to balance the two. I believe it is possible to do great work that we can be proud of even when we come to the very end of our lives and look back.

MY EARLY DREAM OF BEING A SPORTS PHYSIOTHERAPIST

I didn't develop the *Culture Is Everything* approach overnight. While I've always been driven by short- and longer-term dreams to create a positive future, in my early years my goals seemed to come unstuck and my career couldn't get off the ground as I expected. Let me explain.

While I was working my way through a bachelor of physiotherapy degree at the University of Melbourne, my plan was to start my career in a large teaching hospital as a junior physiotherapist, then to become a sports physiotherapist after a few years. My long-term goal was to be treating and working with elite athletes in a busy sports clinic before eventually owning a sports practice of my own, and ultimately to become the physiotherapist for the mighty Richmond Tigers, my favourite Australian rules football team. (Go, Tigers!)

But after five years of university—two spent training in large teaching hospitals—I didn't think I could stomach the idea of another few years in the public hospital system. I now realise that the reason I couldn't handle that public-hospital career direction was because it was in conflict with my Five Beliefs of Meaningful Work. Hospitals have very strict practices with little room for freedom, which I've discovered is an important factor in enjoying my work.

So with a fair bit of apprehension about the whole thing, I skipped forward on the career plan by a few years and took on the challenge of working in a busy private practice in Gippsland, Victoria, as my first physiotherapy job—mostly working with clients who were 80 to 90 percent functioning in their overall lives and needed help to get back to 100 percent.

But after about eleven months, I had to admit that there was a problem—a big one.

I didn't find the work as rewarding as I'd hoped. I was spending all day, every day, in a small physiotherapy treatment room, and every twenty to thirty minutes a new patient would come in to see me. Because of their injuries, many patients were frustrated or angry; as an eternally optimistic person, it was becoming a real challenge to be continuously surrounded by people in a negative frame of mind. Most nights and every weekend I was drained and exhausted and desperately trying to keep up with paperwork. Plus, other than minor injuries barely affecting their everyday lives, the clients were in good health and able to do most of the things they needed or wanted to do. I was starting to question if that type of work really did inspire me. Effectively, I was helping healthy people be even more healthy.

As I reflect on that time, I most certainly did not feel I was helping others in a useful way or feeling proud of the work I was doing, again conflicting with my Five Beliefs of Meaningful Work. And as much as I desperately wanted my career to be in sports physiotherapy, I really didn't enjoy working nights and weekends in order to be where the athletes were—at evening training sessions and weekend footy matches for a local football club. Plus, I didn't find much satisfaction in the outcomes for patients who were already high functioning; I didn't feel as useful as I could be.

I didn't want to admit to myself, let alone anyone else, that I was rethinking my dream. Up until this point, I really thought that I would position myself as an expert in the part of the profession that was the most recognised by people outside the industry: the person that elite athletes would consult after they'd injured themselves playing sport.

Oddly enough, in that first year I found a lot of satisfaction working with the few elderly clients that I had at the practice. Sometimes I found I could help these clients experience as much as 50 percent improvement in their quality of life. For example, if a patient couldn't walk independently to their dining room or the bathroom without lots of pain and discomfort, I was sometimes able to help them regain their mobility to where they could walk those distances with ease. That was rewarding! I found that the elderly people were much more appreciative of the work that I was doing with them. I had been sheepish about working with the elderly—they're not the sexy clientele one thinks of when they think 'physical therapy'. But I remember thinking how the elderly people I was working with were once a much younger, fitter generation of people, and they deserved to be respected and helped to have the most independence.

In short, what I thought I wanted to do wasn't what I really enjoyed doing, and so my head and my heart were telling me to go in two different directions.

After one year, I gave back the keys to the company car, left that dream private-practice / sports-medicine job and moved back home to my parents' house. I'd spent five years at university and one year starting my dream career. Now I didn't have a job, I didn't know where I was headed, and I thought it was going to take me a few years to recover and sort myself out.

RETHINKING MY CAREER PLAN

At home at my parents' place in Foster, Victoria, I reflected on what I had enjoyed as a physio student, which parts of my year in private practice I'd liked the most and what were the coming trends for healthcare in Australia. From this, I realised that I really liked working with elderly folk *and* that there was a phenomenal amount of future demand for physiotherapists in aged care. So I started exploring elderly care as my first step in rebuilding my career.

I got a job working twelve hours per week as a subcontractor physiotherapist at an aged-care home in Preston, an Inner Northern suburb of Melbourne. On first glance, it didn't look like a very nice place—it was old and smelly—but I ended up loving it. That turned out to be one of the most rewarding jobs I've ever had. I felt more empowered to actually make a difference in people's lives. The job also gave me a chance to get to *know* people; instead of a small number of twenty- or thirty-minute consultations with private-practice clients over a few weeks, I could spend time with each of the aged-care home's residents over longer periods. I learnt to understand their needs and their wants, and then tailor my physiotherapy approach to them.

I also enjoyed getting to know the clients' families and the other members of the staff at the aged-care home. I felt like I was part of a caring group of people who worked together to help a group of elderly residents. It felt great and I was inspired! Every day I came to work with a smile on my face because I felt a sense of belonging and like I was doing something useful in the world.

During the first few months working at the Preston nursing home, I was able to build a strong relationship with their director of nursing, and this resulted in me being introduced to management at some nearby aged-care facilities. In a learn-by-the-seat-of-your-pants approach to relationship building and business development, I began meeting with and winning contracts as a physiotherapy supplier to a number of other aged-care homes. By the end of that first year, I was working forty to fifty hours per week at four different aged-care homes. In less than twelve months, I had created a rewarding job that I loved and had more aged-care homes to service than I was able to deliver by myself. With elderly residents to be helped, I saw no other option but to recruit some other people to help me out and join in the fun. So I started employing physiotherapists! That's when, in 2004, my new job became a business and The Physio Co was born.

WHY THIS BOOK?

I've written this book because I want you to understand how we've created a great place to work at The Physio Co. I also want to help you do the same. Creating a great place to work that inspires you and those around you is not only possible but can be much simpler than you might think. This book is to help you learn the steps of a repeatable system to build a strong culture and to give you the confidence to make it happen. I even have a checklist for you to use as you go!

So, my reasons for writing this book are threefold: (1) I want to share my story with you. That story is one that demonstrates that if you're true to your beliefs, it's possible to find purpose and passion no matter where you work (even in aged care!). (2) I'd like to share an insider's view of the TPC family with the outside world. I want the world to recognise the great work that our team does with our clients. (3) I would like to teach and inspire you to have the confidence in this tried-and-tested system of building a great culture and put it to work for yourself.

The *Culture Is Everything* approach isn't just for the touchy-feely physios of TPC. This is a process for successful, numbers-driven entrepreneurial businesses. Read the story here, adopt the system at your workplace and enjoy creating a world-class culture that becomes one of the best places to work!

THE CULTURE IS
EVERYTHING SYSTEM

AS THE FOUNDER AND CEO (chief enthusiasm officer) of a business that has been ranked eight times as one of Australia's Best Places to Work, the questions I most often get from other leaders, managers, business owners and future team members is 'How do you guys do it? How do you create a great culture?'

I used to answer this question by launching into a long explanation that made sense to me but that others found hard to follow.

Since then, I've summarised the approach we use to building a great culture at The Physio Co into 'The *Culture Is Everything* System: The Four Secrets to Creating a World-Class Culture'.[2]

Those four *Culture Is Everything* secrets are:

1. Discover the Core
2. Document the Future
3. Execute Relentlessly
4. Show More Love

---

2   'The Four Secrets to Creating a World Class Culture' is the speech that I most often present to audiences at industry conferences, in-house workshops and company retreats. As a gift to you for reading this book, I've put together a very special readers-only presentation of this speech. Please head over to tristanwhite.com.au/foursecrets if you'd like to see it.

These four secrets are interrelated:

- First, we need to know who we are (**discover the core**) and where are we going (**document the future**);

- Second, to create a great business we need to both **execute relentlessly** and **show more love**. Growing a profitable business fast and simultaneously showing love to your team is not easy. It takes discipline and a robust system to follow.

To be even more practical, I've also created the *Culture Is Everything* Checklist. This one-page checklist defines all nineteen steps that The Physio Co has used to build a world-class culture that is the basis for becoming Australia's Best Place to Work.

Ideally, the checklist would be implemented in sequential order, from one to nineteen. However, the important bit is getting each step embedded, so it can actually be done in any order you choose. In my experience of building one of Australia's Best Places to Work, you need them all.

WHY A CHECKLIST?

Checklists are one of the most valuable tools in business (and in life). Sticking to a checklist with great discipline helps you avoid mistakes. The chance of error is much lower if you follow a tried-and-tested checklist that's purpose-built for the task you are trying to achieve. Checklists work when we set our egos aside, accept human fallibility and follow a system that works. A world-class culture is the foundation of any team that aspires to build a great place to work—'build' being the operative word. Use my *Culture Is Everything* Checklist to build culture in your workplace. You can grab a copy of the checklist right now from tristanwhite. com.au/checklist.

Where to Start

The simplest way to use the *Culture Is Everything* Checklist is to start at the top and move through the list in sequence. But you can start anywhere. You could start near the bottom to find some quick wins that move you towards your very own great place to work.

But Don't Rush It!

To get the best results, take the time to plan, review, communicate, educate and gradually integrate the nineteen steps into your business. I recommend working through the four sections, starting at the top of the checklist and integrating one section per quarter year. That way, it will take a full twelve months to have the systems in place that are the foundations of a great place to work.

The checklist is made up of ideas and best practices that I've learned from the first thirteen years leading The Physio Co. Some of the steps are of our own creation, while others are from people much smarter than I (whom I've done my best to credit throughout the book).

The part that I've played in creating the *Culture Is Everything* Checklist is years of learning, plenty of mistakes and now a summary of the bits that have worked at TPC.

The next ten chapters work through the four secrets and nineteen steps in the checklist to guide you from what's most important to start first, to getting it right and working in the details over time. To first *Discover the Core,* we set our core purpose (chapter 1) and core values (chapters 2 and 3). Then we *Document the Future,* setting a ten-year long-term target (chapter 4) and focusing in with a three-year vision (chapter 5). To *Execute Relentlessly,* we get things done in twelve minutes of power (chapter 6) and hire the right people for the job (chapter 7). And as we execute, we also *Show More Love,* both in how we treat employees from their first day on (chapter 8) and how we celebrate our journey together (chapter 9). Finally, we see how all these elements are the CEO's responsibility and can lead to tremendous growth (chapter 10).

By the end of this book, you'll be able to use the checklist's four secrets and nineteen steps to build a great culture for your workplace. You'll have the answer to every entrepreneur's number-one question: 'How do I create a great culture?'

MONEY ISN'T EVERYTHING

When you have a business with more than one person, you need glue to keep people together, to keep managers, employees, suppliers and customers happy, to keep the business successful and growing. If your motto is 'Money is Everything', and money is the glue that holds everyone together, then I wish you the best of luck. In my experience, *Culture Is Everything.*

A strong workplace culture is created by a group of people who choose to work with a business they trust—a business that inspires and challenges them, that treats them fairly and with respect but doesn't take itself too seriously, that celebrates their successes and supports them in tough times, that exists to make a difference in the world and have some fun along the way. A strong workplace culture is created when people share a common purpose and support each other to bring that purpose to life.

The strongest workplace cultures can survive the tough times. Because tough times happen. Global financial crises arrive. Economies slow down. Floods and earthquakes hit. Clients are lost. And, although hopefully not in my business or yours, people die at work. When bad stuff happens, do you want a group of people on your team who only know the good times? A culture that's only been created since you started giving away more perks than the competition? I certainly don't. It's in the tough times that the people who choose to be part of a strong culture individually ask, 'What can I do to help?' and show that together 'we can do it'.

According to some, the way to a great workplace is to offer as many perks as possible. Now, don't get me wrong—offering benefits to team members is important, but I don't agree it's what builds the trust required to be a great place to work. You see, perks create a culture of entitlement, a 'what's in it for me' culture where employees are always expecting more. And unless you have an unlimited amount of money, you can always be 'out-perked'. Any victory is short-lived because a competitor can always offer more. For example, it's popular to give employees a free day off for their birthday. That sounds nice, but what happens when someone offers two days or a whole week off? This approach to building a great workplace via a 'perk-off' with the competition is a never-ending and very slippery slope.

Honestly, do you really want people on your team who only joined because of the perks? When the going gets tough, I reckon the motto of people attracted to a business with a culture of entitlement built on perks is 'I'm outta here'. Like it or not, a black-swan event will hit. Not if, but when. Will perks matter then?

What do you think: Is it perks or purpose that create a great place to work?

CULTURE IS EVERYTHING
SECRET #1

DISCOVER THE CORE

CHAPTER 1

A SHORT AND EASY-TO-UNDERSTAND CORE PURPOSE
(Instead of a Wishy-Washy Mission Statement)

AS A YOUNG PHYSIO, just one year after graduating from the University of Melbourne and planning to build my career as a sports physiotherapist, I found my true inspiration in the most unlikely of places: an old and smelly home for elderly people in Melbourne's Inner Northern suburb of Preston. That's where I met a resident who inspired me and eventually became my friend—a bloke called George (who, thirteen years on from the first time we met, has a room named after him at The Physio Co's South Melbourne support office).

George lived in that smelly old aged-care home because he had reached a point in his eighties where his legs would no longer work the way he wanted them to and he needed more care than could be managed at home. Before moving into the aged-care home, George had lived at home with his wife, Mavis, just a few blocks away. In spite of his condition, George's dream was to get his legs working again so he could move back and return to Mavis.

As a physiotherapist, I worked with George three times every week, and he would work very hard. We'd practice his walking within a set of parallel bars, we'd do squats, calf raises and lots of other strengthening and balance exercises. Mavis visited the home almost every day, and sometimes while we had our therapy sessions. Over time, I got to know them both.

After our therapy sessions, I'd wheel George back to his room in his wheelchair, and he'd get in bed and rest a little. Often he'd get back in his wheelchair late in the afternoon and wheel himself down the corridor of the care home to the front reception. There he would use the pay phone to call Mavis and chat about their family, his favourite football team (the Essendon Bombers) and the horses that he liked at the races (he loved to have a fifty-cent bet!). Connection to Mavis and the world outside the care home was critical to George and really drove him in his dream of moving home.

George never made it home to live permanently, but one year he was well enough to go home on Christmas Eve and spend a couple of nights at home with his wife, children and grandchildren. I've never seen a more excited eighty-something year-old person than George in the weeks leading up to that Christmas, when he knew he would be spending it at home. And for at least two months afterwards, he recalled stories of his visit home—he would tell me all about it while we did our physio sessions together.

In short, he was the most excitable bloke because he was working towards a dream, and as a physiotherapist, I was able to share that dream with him.

Enthusiasm like I found in George is the reason that I loved working at that aged-care home and the reason that I continue to work in aged care today. Years later, looking back, I realise that working with George was how I discovered what eventually became TPC's core purpose.

DISCOVERING TPC'S CORE PURPOSE

The reason I tell you about George is because that's what TPC does. We help seniors stay mobile, safe and happy. That's our cause. That's our belief. That's what we stand for. That's The Physio Co's core purpose.

A core purpose is the reason an organisation exists. It's a brief statement that anyone can read and think, *Yep, got it. I know exactly what they're up to.* The fewer words the better. For example, Facebook's core purpose is 'to build a global community'. With over 1.86 billion active users every month, Facebook uses their core purpose to continuously pursue their dream to make the world more open and connected.

I first learned of the idea of a core purpose from my favourite business book of all time: *Good to Great*, by Jim Collins. In *Good to Great*, Collins describes how greatness is not a result of chance or circumstance but is largely a matter of conscious choice and discipline. That point was super important to me because it helped me realise that I too had the potential to build a truly great company if I was willing to do the work.

Collins's research has found that a core purpose, or what you stand for, is a critical part of building a team that achieves long-term success. According to him, there are five important characteristics of a good core purpose:

- It absolutely has to be inspiring to those *inside* the organisation.

- It has to be something that could be as valid a hundred years from now as it is today.

- It should help you think expansively about what you *could* do but aren't doing.

- It should help you decide what *not* to do.

- It has to be truly authentic to your company. (Teams that fail on this important point are often the ones that really don't stand for anything and never will.)

Before I read *Good to Great* and discovered the idea of a core purpose, TPC was foundationless. It was impossible for anyone to succinctly know exactly what was important to us, and even I, the founder, was confused and couldn't clearly communicate the reason we existed.

In those pre-core purpose years, I had been drafting various versions of what TPC's vision and mission statements could be. I wasn't creating them to inspire others or to help us decide what to do, as Collins suggested. Instead, I was creating them because I thought that a business wasn't a real business until it had both mission and vision statements! To be completely honest, at that stage I didn't understand the difference between mission and vision, I didn't know why they were important, and I certainly didn't connect with the idea of making them useful for TPC.

A core purpose is more succinct, clear and powerful than either a vision or mission statement (possibly because a lot of vision and mission statements are wishy-washy and effectively meaningless).

Even though a core purpose is short—the length of a single sentence—and the concept is straightforward, it wasn't easy for me to define for TPC. It took me close to a year to draft, redraft, get feedback, think some more, start again, get more feedback and finally cut our core purpose down from about fifteen words to the eight words it is today:

The Physio Co exists *'to help seniors stay mobile, safe and happy'*.

From George to now, that's what TPC has always done and what we'll do for the next hundred years.

HOW A CORE PURPOSE HAS HELPED

In the years since finalising and sharing TPC's core purpose, those eight words have become amazingly powerful in aligning our team and growing our business. In my experience, a core purpose has helped provide a filter to what we should and shouldn't choose to do.

For example, every year, TPC's physiotherapists provide hundreds of thousands of consultations to people just like George (and Mavis) across Australia. Physiotherapy for senior residents of aged-care facilities, retirement villages and private homes is our thing. The Physio Co's core purpose of helping seniors stay mobile, safe and happy makes decision making simple. No, we don't work with young people or athletes—that's not within the scope of our core purpose.

TPC's core purpose is *sticky*. I roll off our core purpose many times every day. I use the core purpose in one-to-one conversations, in all-company updates, in presentations, meetings, interviews, e-mails, training sessions and all sorts of other places. I also ask questions of others about whether what we are doing fits our core purpose. If something aligns with our core purpose, we usually do it. If it doesn't fit, we don't do it. It becomes a very simple filter.

The power of a compelling core purpose is in the simplicity and direction it can provide when used in decision making every day. When referring to TPC's core purpose, potential team members immediately know that physiotherapy for seniors is our thing. Just as importantly, our clients love that we are completely focused on seniors and not trying to be everything to everyone.[3]

Once you have your core purpose, you'll need core values to fully discover your core.

END-OF-CHAPTER CHECKLIST

When putting together the *Culture Is Everything* Checklist, I agonised over whether vision should come before purpose. Because surely an entrepreneurial journey starts with vision, right? Well as much as I wanted to believe that, it's just not true. Purpose comes first. Meaning comes first. My early career discovery that I was more passionate about working with elderly people was the key. I couldn't have figured out a vision if I didn't have that meaning first. That's why Secret #1 is Discover the Core and Secret #2 is Document the Future.

✓ An easy-to-understand core purpose (instead of a wishy-washy mission statement) is step one on the *Culture Is Everything* Checklist.

✓ Step two on the checklist: 'Can *every* team member recite your core purpose?'

---

3   After most speaking engagements where I refer to TPC's core purpose multiple times, many of the audience can remember that TPC exists to help seniors stay mobile, safe and happy just as well as the TPC team. It works!

CORE PURPOSE: TEAM MEMBER STORY

One of the longest-serving TPC team members, who joined TPC in 2005, is a wonderful person called Shilpa. Like me, Shilpa had the pleasure of knowing and working with George at that Preston nursing home. She first joined TPC as a part-time physiotherapist. Since then, she has grown into a very capable team leader, managing a team of TPCers in Melbourne's East. Shilpa leads with her heart. She embraces TPC's core purpose of helping seniors stay mobile, safe and happy and applies it to everything she can—especially the way she cares for her team and her clients.

CHAPTER 2

THREE TO FIVE CORE VALUES THAT INSPIRE GREAT BEHAVIOUR

AS A YOUNG PHYSIO who fell into a career as an entrepreneur, I had, and still have, an overwhelming desire to do what I believe is the right thing—to make decisions and actions that I am proud of and that I would happily explain to my Mum or publish for the whole world to know.

There are plenty of people who may initially think that this 'do the right thing' approach is far too idealistic or even outright crazy. But it turns out that doing the right thing to show that you care, that you are authentic, and that you are sticking to your core values can work over the long term—Jim Collins's research confirmed it.

Leading a business or team is an opportunity to do something meaningful in the world. Leading by consistently doing the right thing, in my experience, is a surefire way to achieve long-term success, with loyal clients and long-term team members.

There is a direct link between my desire to do the right thing and the third of my Five Beliefs of Meaningful Work: I believe we enjoy work when we feel proud of doing the right thing in challenging situations.

PEOPLE CAN'T READ MY MIND!

It turned out it was easier to do what I thought was the right thing myself than it was to empower others to do the same. Reading other people's minds is not a skill that I have, and I don't know anyone who can read my mind, either. At times I felt frustrated as our team grew and our team members, although doing their best, weren't behaving in the way I had hoped. But they couldn't read my mind, so what else could I expect?

It wasn't until I read Verne Harnish's book, *Mastering the Rockefeller Habits,* that I discovered the power of using core values to guide the behaviour of my teammates. As a leader, I realised I had to become passionate about providing clear communication to my team that would set them up for success. But I really struggled with providing the *right* direction on the behaviours that I expected *and* allowing each team member the freedom to also bring their own thoughts, ideas and personal flair to the job.

It was then that I realised a set of three to five core values could become our playbook for success in aligning the right behaviours in our team.

THE FOUNDATIONS OF A GREAT CULTURE

In 2009, when I began to understand what it meant to have a culture by design (as opposed to a culture that occurs by default because no one is paying attention to it), I realised I needed to discover core values and begin using TPC-specific language to clarify what we were doing and where we were going.

To discover TPC's core values, I took a two-week break from work and reflected on what was important to us and how those behaviours could be documented in a clear and inspiring way. It's important to note that the core values were *discovered*, not created. The behaviours and beliefs that underpinned how TPCers act were already loosely understood; it was the documenting of these beliefs into actionable words that had been the missing step.

The TPC core values took quite a long time to craft; like our core purpose, I discussed many drafts with a small number of teammates before I felt we had arrived at the right words to make them short, sharp and memorable.

TPC'S CORE VALUES

I was very careful with the language for the core values, and each of the four values was crafted as an action. For example, one TPC value is not merely 'Respect' but 'Respect Everyone'. To live that value, you actually have to do something—an important aspect of living, breathing core values.

Each TPC core value is an action statement that then has more detail of the behaviours associated with that value; the beauty of this is that the details reveal exactly what we expect of our team members. Today, these values provide us all with guidance for making decisions and taking action.

TPC's four core values are

- Respect Everyone;

- Be Memorable;

- Find a Better Way; and

- Think Big, Act Small.

Every day, we work to achieve our goals by consistently living these values. Any decision, problem or issue is answered by referring to them. As with our core purpose, I repeat our core values frequently in conversations, meetings and interviews.

Interestingly, and a bit embarrassingly, about six months after TPC's core values were released to our team and I had started using them in as many conversations and documents as I possibly could, it occurred to me that the values assigned to my business were effectively my own personal core values. I was initially shocked and then a bit embarrassed, but finally I accepted that alignment was probably inevitable—and desirable—and embraced the values even more.

To give you a better sense of why core values are important for your business, let me run you through the core values of TPC and how we live them every day in every interaction possible.

RESPECT EVERYONE

Our first core value, 'Respect Everyone', is about understanding that a small thing on our list of priorities may be the *only* thing that matters to an elderly client. This means the following:

- We are always on time.

- We always do what we say we will do.

- We always communicate in clear, concise and honest ways.

- We are generous with our time to help others.

In aged care, some of the best therapy that TPCers can provide is simply to smile, stop, chat and listen. That in itself can inspire a resident to do something she never thought she could, or to keep doing her exercises so that she can, for example, keep walking to exercise class.

Our team members also know that they must be respectful of every client's time. If a TPCer has an appointment with a resident at 2:00 p.m., it may be the most important thing happening in that resident's day. If the physio doesn't show on time, it can be very disappointing for that resident—disappointing enough that it actually impacts the therapy session. That's why it's so important that we are on time, or if there's a chance that we're going to be late, that we communicate that fact in a clear, concise and honest way.

This is an example of how even a small act of just showing up on time can be extremely special to someone else. That individual is going to pay you back by working hard and trying to do what you instruct—there will be mutual respect.

BE MEMORABLE

Our next core value, 'Be Memorable', is about setting high standards, having great attention to detail and wanting to impress. This means the following:

- We are friendly and make positive first impressions.

- We make people smile with our personal and understanding approach.

- We take the time to celebrate milestones and successes.

- We wow people whenever possible.

We believe in starting the day with a positive demeanor to not only make our day happier but to make everyone we come in contact with happier. We often joke that the TPC uniform includes two key components: a name badge and a smile. Smiles, we've found, are infectious, and using a smile to start a therapy session helps to release endorphins, which usually results in a more positive interaction right from the start.

Being memorable is also about taking the time to celebrate milestones and successes. While TPCers do this for residents, we also do this within the TPC family. For instance, we send a card and a personal, handwritten note to each TPC team member twice a year: on a member's birthday and his or her anniversary with TPC.

Perhaps one of the most misunderstood parts of our core values is 'We wow people whenever possible'. I've spoken with TPCers who were actually a little frightened that they might not be able to 'wow' someone because they were not comfortable being overly loud or acting like 'the life of the party'. However, it can be the seemingly insignificant acts such as remembering the name of a family member when talking with one of our residents or dropping in more often to visit a resident who is feeling lonely—these are 'wows' that make a difference to our residents.

Sometimes it's the smallest acts that have the biggest impact.

FIND A BETTER WAY

This core value, 'Find a Better Way', is about the fact that complacency is not our thing. This means the following:

- We always search for new ways that help our clients, customers and team members.

- We are committed to constantly improving, personally and collectively.

- We inspire others by continually finding a better way.

We're obsessed with being better tomorrow than we are today. We talk about improving every single day, even if it's only by 1 percent.

From the moment new hires join the TPC family, they're reminded that they have a voice just like any other TPC team member, and if they see anything they think could be improved so that our residents, our clients (or facilities) or our team can have better outcomes, we ask them to please share those ideas because we're a much smarter group of people when we're all contributing.

I felt that 'Find a Better Way' was so important that a few years back I actually set a key performance indicator for myself that I would publicly share something that I tried and didn't get quite right (but learnt from) every single week. We all make mistakes, but we don't all have to make the same mistakes. If we share them so that only one of us has to make that mistake, then I think we're a smarter and stronger organisation because of it.

Here again, this core value goes beyond assisting our aged-care residents and bettering TPC. We also believe in finding better ways to help TPCers in their personal lives. For instance, if we can make it so that someone doesn't have to drive as far to get to work in order to spend more time with his or her young family, or if a job share will improve a TPCer's quality of life outside of his or her time at work, then we certainly do our very best to make that happen.

THINK BIG, ACT SMALL

Finally, with this core value, 'Think Big, Act Small', we are essentially reminding ourselves that 'We are David, not Goliath'. This means the following:

- We are always prepared to 'give it a go'.

- We are nimble, flexible and easygoing.

- We always ask: 'What can I do next?'

- We all help to achieve our Painted Picture of the future.

Team members don't always equate their acts to 'thinking big', but here again, they may not realise the power of stopping in to say hello to someone or maybe leaving a small handwritten note. They often don't equate these small gestures as being backed by big thinking.

What this core value is really about is that there's never a time for just twiddling our thumbs. There's always something to be done, but we must seek it out ourselves and be proactive. People often think it's interesting that we include the word 'nimble' in our core values. We use that because we like to think that we're responsive to any situation.

The last part of this core value, 'We all help to achieve our Painted Picture of the future', represents the fact that none of us is a lone wolf—we all are part of an organisation that is expected to continue to grow both the business and our service (more about the Painted Picture in chapter 5). Every TPCer pulls his weight by living the core values and helping the organisation move forward.[4]

VALUES ALIGNMENT

TPC was five years old when we documented and communicated its core values. At that stage, we had approximately twenty team members. Up until the moment the values were shared, our team members had not been held accountable to a set of behaviours or

---

4   Despite the direction these core values provide, conflicts in decision making can occur that require team members to carefully think through their actions. For example, as part of the 'Respect Everyone' core value, TPCers are reminded that 'We are always on time' AND that 'We are generous with our time to help others'. If we do both of those things simultaneously, then we might not always be on time, because we're being generous with our time to help others. The way this conflict is resolved is using the guidance of another part of TPC's Respect Everyone core value: 'We always communicate in clear, concise and honest ways'. As part of our training of new TPCers, these conflicts are identified and examples given on how to resolve.

core values. In effect, the behavioural goalposts shifted at that very moment.

That was a challenge for all of us but especially for three of the twenty existing team members. I worked closely with everyone to ensure we could effectively align ourselves to the values, but for those three there was a misalignment between their personal values and the newly implemented TPC values.

As it became clear that TPC was committed to living our core values and the misalignment kept recurring with these three TPCers, they each in their own time decided it was best to move on and find a new professional home where they were more suited. That was not an easy time for TPC, these three team members or me as a still twenty-something physiotherapist-turned-entrepreneur.

END-OF-CHAPTER CHECKLIST

✓ Three to five core values that every team member can remember is step 3 on the *Culture Is Everything* Checklist.

CORE VALUES: TEAM MEMBER STORY

A TPCer named Kelly joined TPC as a graduate Physio, and now she's progressed into a position as a team leader. When she was working as a physiotherapist, she was consulting a resident who had a collection of porcelain dolls in her room. The resident just loved her porcelain-doll collection, but she was a bit upset that one of them had been bumped onto the floor and had broken. Kelly told her she didn't know if she could do it, but she wanted to take the doll and see if she could get it fixed.

While Kel couldn't fix the doll herself, her fiancé, Karl, was good with his hands and was recruited for the repair job! So with some glue and patience, Karl was able to repair the doll. It was almost as good as new when Kel took it back to the resident at the aged-care home. The result: the resident was rapt! She gave Kel a big smile and hug when she saw her doll had been fixed. This beautiful example of TPC's 'Be Memorable' core value in action built an even stronger connection between Kelly and her client.

CHAPTER 3

SHARING CORE VALUE STORIES
TO REWARD, RECOGNISE
AND REEDUCATE

I LIKE SIMPLICITY. In fact, I believe it is the job of a leader to make the complex task of managing a team as simple as possible for everyone. One of the simplest and most powerful ways I've discovered to make my job and that of my team members as simple as possible is to use core values in almost everything we do. If ever we are stuck or unsure of what we should do, we refer to our core values and use them to guide us.

This choice, to be a values-based business, results in a commitment that core values become the basis of everything. That includes recruitment, selection, training, reward and recognition, language, celebrations, performance reviews and everything else.

My favourite book for first-time managers to read is *The One Minute Manager*. This little book teaches the importance of catching people doing something right (as opposed to only when they notice something going wrong).

The combination of this focus on catching others doing something right and our commitment to our core values is the basis of TPC's reward-and-recognition program.

The Physio Co core values are reflected in our MVP program, in our website and in our Painted Picture vision. They are also used in recruitment, and we share stories of TPCers living our values at 'To the Point' daily huddles.

Sharing stories of team members living core values and then celebrating their successes is one of the best ways I've found to speak a consistent language and to reward, recognise and reeducate others in their efforts to be an aligned team.

Core value lived: Find a Better Way (We inspire others by continually finding a better way.)

Nominated by: Michael

Who lived it: Maryan

How was the value lived: 'TPC physio Maryan had an elderly client that she'd been working with who had slipped over and was in desperate need of some new shoes with better grip. Maryan went shopping in her own time and with her own money to buy some new shoes for this resident, who didn't have any family or friends to do it for her. The brand-new shoes made the resident feel very special, and of course she's now much safer on her feet. Thanks, Maryan, you've inspired us all to continue finding a better way!'

TPC MVP PROGRAM

Have you ever been inside a McDonald's or KFC restaurant and noticed a plaque on the wall celebrating the restaurant's employee of the month? If so, you will understand the TPC Most Valuable Person (MVP) program. Effectively, the MVP program is an employee-of-the-month program based on living our core values. Every month, a TPC MVP is selected, and in December the MVP of the Year is selected from those monthly winners and celebrated. Let me explain.

We use TPC's four core values as the basis for the selection criteria for the monthly MVP, and we ask TPC team members to nominate a peer who they feel is living a core value exceptionally well. Every TPCer is expected to nominate at least one other person for living a TPC value each month. We also allow TPCers to nominate themselves. Every month, we call for nominations; in 2016 approximately a hundred nominations were received each month.

We publicly present MVP awards for TPCers nominated for living the core values, we announce four finalists and then one MVP in a fun and kind-of-silly storytelling ceremony. I get to do quite a few of the announcements, and I really enjoy being able to stand in front of the TPC family and not only recognise people who have done some great work but also add some energy to the event. First I explain the reward-and-recognition program to the entire team so that any new hires understand what's happening. I explain that there will be four finalists from among those nominated and ask that the finalists please bound onto the stage with lots of energy when their name is called. Then, one by one, we call out the finalists' names, and they launch onto the stage and share high fives with me and with Jess, our creator of energy and inspiration, who helps with the MVP ceremony.

We applaud all the nominees, and then I get to tell the story of why each finalist was nominated for living a core value, with a round of applause for each. It's quite ceremonious and high energy.

After we announce the finalists, we have a big drum roll— everyone in the crowd drums their knees or the seat in front of them with their hands. It gets noisy!

Then we announce via the screen in front of everyone the MVP. This is the signal for a big cheer and a big celebration before we hand out the awards. That ceremony and the recognition given to our hard-working team is one of my favourite parts of being CEO; I like to think I'm recognising great work from our team, rewarding people for their effort and reinforcing the important behaviours that define the TPC way.

Each person who made the nomination of a finalist or MVP is also publicly recognised as part of the MVP-awards process. So all told, eight TPCers are publicly recognised each month, and the finalists and MVP each receive a voucher.

The MVP of the Year is a highly sought-after prize. The winner is announced in front of the entire team as well as all the spouses, partners, children and other family members who came with them to the Christmas party. It's a huge honour to be announced TPC's MVP of the Year (more about the Christmas party in chapter 8).

Altogether, forty-eight finalists win a $25 voucher each year. The twelve monthly MVPs win a $100 voucher, and the MVP of the Year wins a $500 voucher (and bragging rights for twelve months!).

REINFORCING GREAT BEHAVIOUR

Part of the reason for creating the MVP program was for all of us to really think about what we're doing and to capture these moments in time that are so interesting and so inherently rewarding—and such a big part of why we continue to work in this industry.

The MVP awards ceremony is a way to dig deep into the TPC family and into the individual interactions that people are doing on a daily basis. Being able to recognise and document those tasks says that, yes, TPC is making progress, but it's only because we've got people who are committed to every conversation and every treatment session. By creating a communication platform that allows us to recognise and talk about those individual interactions, which is what we're talking about with the MVP awards, brings it back to how we can all contribute to TPC's progress.

So it's the small things that comprise the big thing, which is our company's future.

To demonstrate how nominations for MVP awards recognise TPCers for doing things that represent the core values, as an example of the 'Be Memorable' core value 'We make people smile with our personal and understanding approach', TPCer Mel was nominated by TPCer Amanda, who reported that:

'Mel discovered that a resident loved the *Anne of Green Gables* books, but due to decreased vision she could no longer read them. Mel, being the lovely person she is, brought in her own copy of the book and has started a ritual of reading it to the resident as part of a chronic pain management program. Now all of the physios that see this resident are reading it to her, so she gets to listen to her favourite book, which puts a smile on both her and the physio's face. Thanks, Mel, for starting this; it gives joy to all of us that participate.'

Another example of sharing our values being lived is how our creator of energy and inspiration e-mails at least one TPCer every day to say, 'You've been nominated for living a TPC value!' This chirpy little e-mail lets someone know he or she has been nominated for exceptional work and recognised with an MVP nomination that has been shared at that day's To the Point huddle (the morning central-office update meeting, which I'll discuss more in chapter 6). With one per day (five per week), more than 250 of these positive little e-mails are sent to deserving team members every year.

The MVP awards ceremony has been a regular part of the TPC culture since 2009, and it has turned into quite a big 'to do' with many nominations, in part because of the expectation that everyone will nominate a peer.

But the program wasn't always this way. When we first launched it in 2009, there were only a very small number of nominations of people living the core values because we were still figuring them out and getting familiar with them. In fact, early in the program I remember one month where there were only one or two nominations, and I personally had to make a couple of nominations so that we had at least four finalists. After that, I really began encouraging others to make nominations.

Over time, TPCers began taking pride in seeing the person that they had nominated getting up on stage and receiving an award, and then there began to be a lot of camaraderie in actually being the person that nominated the winner for the MVP award. So it's been a journey getting the program going and arriving at where we are with it today.

STORYTELLING AROUND CORE VALUES

A crucial part of a strong team culture is the commitment of a group of people who live and believe in a small set of shared values. Businesses based on living a set of core values often have the very best workplace cultures. And the beauty of core values is that you can use them in nearly every part of your business.

Therefore, growing a values-based organisation is about attracting more and more people who share those values. The way those values are lived every day is what builds the strong culture. **Importantly, the very smallest gesture that lives a core value can make the biggest impact.**

At The Physio Co, we use storytelling around our core values in as many conversations as we possibly can. For example, every day at our daily huddle, one member of our support team shares a short, one-minute story of a team member living one of our four core values. Positive stories of teammates getting great results and being recognised by their peers is fun, feels great and helps to focus everyone on what works.

Storytelling is without doubt *the* best way to build and strengthen a strong culture. No matter how many stories you're already telling, I reckon you can always tell more!

At The Physio Co, one of our core values is 'Be Memorable', which guides us to be 'friendly and make positive first impressions'. One small way that our team lives this value is in our e-mails. Since 2009, The Physio Co support team have all had 'Have a great day' as the way we sign off from every e-mail. This very small change from 'Kind regards' has had a huge impact. People continue to notice it, mention it and associate it with The Physio Co. Eight years on, these four words continue to live our 'Be Memorable' value and reinforce to everyone that we are a positive and welcoming family.

ENDURING STORIES FROM THE EARLY DAYS

New stories are created every day, and it's critical that those stories are shared. However, it's often the stories from the very early days of a business that last the longest.

Recording, immortalising and retelling the stories from the start-up days of your business could be the most powerful way to build a strong culture (and it's never too late to start). At The Physio Co, each room in our South Melbourne support office tells a story from the early days. For example, the George Garraway Room immortalises the memory of the elderly resident from the very first aged-care home we ever visited—the old and smelly home in Preston—who got to go home on Christmas Eve and whose story opens chapter 1. The John D Rockefeller Room tells the story of our commitment to simplifying our business and to the Rockefeller Habits. Naming rooms is just one way to tell stories and bring the past to life.

Over the last few years, I've started writing a regular letter to each member of The Physio Co family that's posted in the mail and sent to their homes. This letter is another great opportunity to tell stories from the early days.

The Physio Co Museum is yet to be opened; however, every year we are collecting as much history as we can, including photos, old posters, logos, business cards, awards, t-shirts, name badges, and anything else we can remember. One day we will immortalise it all in our very own museum. In the meantime, telling stories is one of the most powerful ways to remember the past, and we do that as often as possible.

SHOWING RECOGNITION EVERY DAY

As I learned from *The One Minute Manager*, I am forever trying to catch people doing something right. That approach, as opposed to the typical management habit of catching people only when they are doing something wrong, is how our leadership team shows its appreciation every day. When we catch people doing something right, rather than some sort of formal recognition every time, we just express our appreciation directly to the team member, in the moment. It's a very grateful way to go about our work every day.

As managers and leaders, we also do our best to actually involve ourselves (respectfully and only when it's wanted) in people's lives outside of work. For example, a team leader recently went with his wife to an engagement party of a member of his team, where they met the physio's parents and fiancée. The parents were so pleased and proud that this young lad's boss came to the weekend event. As members of the TPC family, we feel it's important to show our TPC team mates how much they mean to us.

Core values and stories of them in action are an amazingly powerful way to recognise and reward great behaviour. Similarly, the use of core-value stories is equally as powerful in reeducating team members who aren't living the values the way their leader might expect. A direct and respectful conversation that uses the core values as a common language can be a super effective way of dealing with what otherwise could be a challenging or uncomfortable conversation. Remember, though, as leaders we need to praise in public and challenge (or reeducate) in private. That's the respectful way to lead.

END-OF-CHAPTER CHECKLIST

- ✓ Are your core values used for a recognition-and-reward program that drives culture?

- ✓ Are your core values used in every team member's quarterly review?

Core value lived: Respect Everyone (We are generous with our time to help others.)

Nominated by: Seon

Who lived it: Kate

How was the value lived: 'Kate has had such a positive impact at Sandfield aged-care home. One example of Kate's commitment to her clients is a story of a lady who has Parkinson's disease. This client had had a hip replacement and was suffering from extreme pain, as well as trying to manage Parkinson's symptoms, still six months post-operation. Kate followed up with doctors and specialists to have the pain reviewed as well as advocating for something to be done to improve how her Parkinson's medication was administered to try and control her symptoms better. With persistence from Kate, the resident's pain was investigated, and a pump was put in to administer the Parkinson's medications. For the first time in six months the resident was able to walk a short distance with Kate outside of her room! There is still a way to go, but with Kate's commitment, the client is now much more mobile, safe and happy.'

CULTURE IS EVERYTHING
SECRET #2

DOCUMENT THE FUTURE

CHAPTER 4

A TEN-YEAR OBSESSION THAT ACTS AS YOUR NORTH STAR

DAYDREAMING ABOUT THE FUTURE is a simple pleasure. I do it often, and I love it. But I rarely stop at the thought of, *One day I'll do that*. Instead, I decide *when* I'd like the dream to come true, and then I work backwards to make it happen.

One dream that I have looks, feels and sounds like this:

It's December 2018, and one of our TPC team members has just performed our *two millionth* client consultation since 2009. I and the 180 team members at TPC are ecstatic. This is the goal we've been working towards for ten years, and we got there!

Working towards the goal meant thousands of hours of hard work planning, leading, organising and delivering. It means that we've done something useful for many, many people—like Betty, who received the two millionth consult.

Betty is typical of a TPC client: in my daydream, she's an eighty-two-year-old lady who has struggled to walk far over the past eighteen months after a nasty fall. She was admitted to an aged-care home, where she was assessed by a TPC physio and received weekly physiotherapy sessions along with a daily exercise program over a three-month period. With all that attention, help and therapy, Betty regained her mobility, her confidence and her big smile!

Betty, as well as the people who received the 1,999,999 consultations before her, is TPC's North Star, our obsession that drives me and our team members every day. Today, TPC is well on its way to achieving our goal, mostly because it is so clearly defined for everyone.

Without that ten-year obsession, where would we ever go? What dream could we ever achieve?

THE FIFTH-YEAR STRUGGLE

Growing The Physio Co into a large team wasn't the culmination of a clear dream for me during the first few years at TPC. I'd set out to find or create a physiotherapy job that inspired me. I'd hoped that once I found that job, I'd also be surrounded by other inspiring people, too. But I didn't realise I'd have to become an entrepreneur to make that happen! Building a business with many moving parts, mostly people, was so far from the physiotherapy job I initially had in mind.

Between 2004 and 2008, the first five years of The Physio Co, I was still getting used to working in aged care and understanding the industry myself, let alone knowing how to lead a fast-growing business.

Through those first five years, TPC didn't have a clear direction. I was a young physiotherapist who had somehow become a small-business owner. With blind enthusiasm and plenty of opportunity in a changing industry, TPC had grown from one person with an idea in 2004 to a team of twenty-odd physiotherapists with a passion for working with seniors. But the organisation was essentially directionless.

From 2004 to 2008, I had grown a business from start-up to a small team of twenty people that was profitable and sustainable, and even won a few awards. From the outside, TPC looked like a thriving practice with a big future. But on the inside, I was feeling frustrated, exhausted and stuck in a job I didn't enjoy. I had built myself a job that meant the entire business relied on me. I was the glue that held the place together. I'd even recruited my sister, my best mate and my fiancée to help me handle the amazing complexity that I'd created for myself! I was working six or seven days a week, was eternally stressed and knew that I couldn't do this forever. I thought owning a business was supposed to be fun!

As a group, those twenty physios and I were delivering about forty thousand consultations per year to elderly people at a small number of Melbourne and regional Victorian aged-care homes. We certainly weren't an aligned team that could work both independently and confidently to make decisions about our future. Instead, we were a reactive group that asked the boss (me) every time there was any slightly out-of-the-ordinary question to deal with. We were far from the cohesive team with a clear core purpose and defined vision that TPC has become.

The main reason for this lack of purpose and direction was because I didn't know anything about that business stuff, let alone did I make time to learn it, apply it and communicate it in the obsessive way I now understand.

In 2009, those twenty team members were reporting to me. My phone rang all day and into the night because I hadn't made it clear to anyone that they could make decisions on their own. Every out-of-the-ordinary request from a client, their family or the aged-care home became a question I had to answer. I wanted our team to be empowered and independent in how they did their jobs so that I could do mine, but I didn't know how to make that happen. As a result, I was feeling amazingly stressed, frustrated and sort of 'stuck'.

After five years, I wasn't enjoying leading a growing team in that haphazard way I'd created. In truth, I really wasn't leading the team because I was continually fielding questions all day long and being completely reactive. I wasn't the caring, supportive and inspiring leader that I now know is needed. Nor was I taking care of residents anymore because I'd become a supervisor of other people. Worse still, I was starting to lose some enthusiasm. I really wanted to get back to my passion, to those earlier rewarding days of helping seniors stay mobile, safe and happy. I'd lost sight of why I started TPC in the first place and where we were headed in the future.

At that point, if I'd had a conversation with you or one of your friends, I would've been very descriptive about the direction of TPC and how I saw it looking in the future, based on doing more of what we had been doing up until then. But a week or two later, I might have described a slightly different outlook in a conversation with someone else. I wasn't being dishonest; I just hadn't decided on a clear vision and made it known to everyone. Therefore, it kept changing. I wasn't consistent with my thinking or the message I was sharing.

This ever-changing vision created a very disjointed group of people; our physiotherapists were passionate about helping the elderly but not clear on why they were doing what they were doing or where we were headed as a team. The same applied to me.

I decided that I either needed to find a solution as to how I could align our growing team and empower everyone to be more independent, or move on and find someone who could do that better than I could.

So in early 2009 I went looking for a solution. One of the methods I discovered, and the one that resonated with me the most, was the concept of a long-term goal to really focus and inspire. This concept has changed TPC and my life forever.

Along with a set of clear core values, Jim Collins wrote in *Good to Great* about the need for a great business to have a long-term vision, something he describes as a Big Hairy Audacious Goal, or BHAG. This huge, sometimes seemingly impossible-to-achieve goal is one that can inspire a group of committed people over a ten- to thirty-year period.

So in mid-2009 we formulated a long-term dream based on Collins's BHAG concept. That concept I now call our ten-year obsession.[5]

That ten-year obsession was, and still is, for the TPC team to deliver two million (yep, 2,000,000!) consultations to Australian aged-care residents by 31 December 2018.

The way the ten-year obsession was created was by both reflecting on the past and gazing into the future to set a goal that scared the hell out of us all. At the time, The Physio Co's twenty-person team was delivering approximately forty thousand client consultations per year and growing that number at close to 100 percent each year.

Then, thanks to an article from one of the member leaders in EO, I read about a type of fast-growing company described as a

---

5   I first learned of the concept of a values-based business when I reached out to Naomi Simson, founding director of RedBalloon, and she suggested I read Verne Harnish's book *Mastering the Rockefeller Habits*. Naomi also suggested I consider joining the peer-to-peer network Entrepreneurs' Organization (EO) to help me learn and grow. As an obsessive learner, I did both of these things and am rapt I did. Thanks, Naomi! Verne and his *Mastering the Rockefeller Habits* approach led me to another author who has become my favourite business writer yet: Jim Collins.

At this point in the book, I need to thank two people who guided me at that time of my life and who have become long-term mentors on my TPC journey: Verne Harnish and Cameron Herold. With the guidance of Verne and Cameron, I discovered the importance of a crystal-clear vision and a set of memorable core values as important building blocks of a thriving culture.

gazelle—growing consistently at 20 percent or more per year. That sounded like the sort of business that excited me. But although I was realistic enough to understand that 100 percent growth each year over a decade was not something we could sustain, 20 percent per year didn't seem exciting enough. Somehow, we figured out that 35 percent growth every year from a starting point of forty thousand would get us to a cumulative total of two million consults in ten years. That plan was good enough for me, and it was set—two million unique and memorable consultations by 31 December 2018.

TPC's ten-year obsession quickly became TPC's North Star. Our guiding light. The starting point of our Painted Picture visions.

The progress towards our ten-year obsession is shared with everyone on the team during every all-company event, keeping everyone up to date on our 'TPC tally'. That tally keeps track of how many consultations we need to achieve during the year, what percentage of the year has passed, and whether we're on track to meet our ten-year goal.

While management provides the support, in order to achieve our goals, every team member needs to understand how the work they do every day contributes to TPC achieving our bigger goals. It's a big task completing two million consultations in only ten years from close to a standing start.

THE POWER OF CLARITY

Today, TPC is five times the size we were when the ten-year obsession was created in 2009. We have a long-term vision, laser focus on the future and exciting career opportunities for our hundred-plus team members. What sets us apart from other businesses is clarity around the future and what it may look like, which is inspiring for current and future team members who want to join us on the journey.

A clear and exciting long-term goal is a starting point for building a sustainable business and a strong culture. But only when that goal is measurable and you track it regularly does it become compelling. A ten-year obsession is your answer.

END-OF-CHAPTER CHECKLIST

✓ Do you have a ten-year obsession that inspires your team culture?

✓ Does every team member get regular updates on progress towards your ten-year obsession?

CHAPTER 5

CREATE YOUR VISION OF SUCCESS: THE THREE-YEAR PAINTED PICTURE

A STRONG CULTURE NEEDS a clear vision. Nearly every person I've ever met has been energised by the thought of being part of a growing organisation that's achieving its goals. But unless you very clearly document and share that vision with everyone, and refer back to it often, it can be easily forgotten.

A ten-year goal or obsession that acts as your North Star is critical for entrepreneurs and leaders if they are planning to create something significant in the world. However, for most employees, ten years is an impossibly long time. It can feel like a lifetime—and far too long to imagine themselves into the future. In fact, planning more than two to three years into the future can be a challenge for many people, particularly new graduates and younger members of a team.

So, to bring The Physio Co's ten-year obsession to life, we worked backwards to determine what would be required each year to eventually achieve that big dream. Once that was determined, the ten-year goal was broken down into manageable segments—three-year goals to start. This allowed us to create a short, engaging description of how TPC's exciting future would evolve.

That document became our first three-year plan, our Painted Picture vision of 2012, created in 2009.

I first learned of the Painted Picture vision idea from business coach Cameron Herold. Cameron described to me how winter Olympic athletes, including the brave souls who compete in the ski jumping events, regularly use this Painted Picture vision concept to visualise in great detail how they will execute the perfect, gold medal-winning jump. They then review their written description over and over and over as they train and plan for success.

By leaning into the future to describe how they will perform and then working obsessively to bring that vision to life, the skiers are attempting to create their own future. As leaders committed to creating a world-class culture, we can use the same approach to lean into the future and describe in detail how our business and culture will look, act and feel on a certain date. Then we take that vision, share it with our team, review it daily and obsess over bringing it to life. That's the concept of a Painted Picture vision.

Another way to think of a Painted Picture vision is to visualise it as a base camp on a journey up a mountain. Jim Collins describes working towards a ten-year goal like climbing a mountain. Mountain climbers don't typically start at the bottom of a mountain like Mt Everest or Mt Kilimanjaro and simply go straight up. They plan the climb and aim for places where they can rest, regroup and plan the next stage. Once the climbers arrive at one of these base camps, they move on to the next. Just like mountain climbers use base camps to scale huge peaks, culture-

focused leaders can use Painted Picture visions
to help achieve their ten-year obsessions.

Let me explain how we use the Painted Picture concept at TPC. Back in 2009, The Physio Co created our first Painted Picture vision of how our business would look, act and feel in three years' time. That first Painted Picture described in detail how The Physio Co would be on 31 December 2012 when we reached our first milestone, on the journey towards the ten-year goal of delivering two million consultations by 2018.

LAUNCHING THE FIRST PAINTED PICTURE

With the Painted Picture vision formulated, I gathered our team of twenty aged-care physios together on a cold, wintry night in Melbourne in mid-2009, and we had the first of what we now call a 'learning event', which is a professional-development or training event. (Today, we have lots of these throughout the year to continuously improve and live our value of 'Find a Better Way'.) That night in 2009, we heard first from an expert presenter on aged-care physio, and then I gave an update on the company from my perspective. That is when I shared our Painted Picture vision for the first time.

Our vision, I shared with enthusiasm and pride, was to deliver two million consultations in ten years, and that we would begin with three shorter-term goals. By 31 December 2012, TPC would

- expand to a team of fifty;

- be delivering a hundred thousand consultations per year; and

- move into the top ten of the 'Best Places to Work in Australia' (from our 37th-place ranking at the time).

I enthusiastically shared those three big goals with the group, and at the end of the presentation I stopped and stood there with a big smile on my face, very proud of this vision.

The trouble was, I was the only person smiling; there was absolute silence from the rest of our team. When I asked, 'Why the silence?' one of them replied that they loved the idea of growth, 'But we're aged-care physios', she said. 'We've got no idea how to do what you're describing for us'.

That feedback was powerful and a little sobering, but my excitement was unwavering. I responded by suggesting that 'If we all agree this is the direction we're headed, then we can get to work on making it happen. We'll have three years to figure out how we're going to do it!'

At that point, there was a collective sigh of relief around the room, and the team member who had raised the question confirmed that as long as there would be support to continue to provide great care, they would continue to do so and help grow TPC.

So for the next three and a half years the TPC team and I obsessed over how to bring that Painted Picture vision to life. Doing that meant continually updating everyone as to how the company was doing and asking for input and help in recruiting the next TPCer for our team.

From 2009 to 2012, we obsessed over bringing that vision to life. Every decision we made was aligned with those goals. Every team member we selected, client we engaged, story we told, Culture Book we published and party we threw was aligned with bringing our vision to life.

During 2012, The Physio Co delivered 108,674 physiotherapy consultations for Australian aged-care residents, we ended that year with fifty-four team members and were ranked as the eigth Best Place to Work in Australia. We hit all three of the key numbers we set back in 2009. There'd been plenty of bumps along the way, but by being committed to our vision we brought it to life. Visit www.thephysioco.com.au/paintedpicture.

USING THE PAINTED PICTURE AS AN OPPORTUNITY TO CELEBRATE

Here is a copy of a letter I posted to the homes of every team member when we reached one of our Painted Picture goals in early 2012:

. . . 'One of the goals in that vision was that by 31 December 2012: **"We have more than fifty fantastic team members that are appreciated for the great work they do."**

Well, today is the day! As of April 11, 2012, The Physio Co family has more than fifty members. Woohoo!! The Physio Co Painted Picture is coming to life.

Welcome to new TPCers May and Adrian, who joined us today and helped us hit our milestone.

Thanks so much to everyone at The Physio Co for believing in our vision and helping bring it to life. We've achieved this goal 264 days early, and it feels fantastic!!

Yep, we've hit our goals and we're celebrating. (TPCers—please check your mailboxes for a little pressie; Jess—thanks for the awesome cake!)

The Physio Co family is a fun and exciting place to work. Stay tuned for even more of our Painted Picture of 2012 goals to come true in the next few months . . .'

HOW TPCERS CONTRIBUTE TO THE PAINTED PICTURE VISIONS

Since the first Painted Picture vision was formulated in 2009, obsessed over for three years and then came to life in 2012, we launched a second Painted Picture vision (2013–2015, the second three years of the ten-year plan), and in early 2016 we released the last of this set of three Painted Picture visions, taking us to our ten-year obsession of 2018. The Painted Picture visions have helped to transform TPC from a directionless group of individuals to a more-aligned and inspired team. We're now on track to achieve our goal of two million consultations, and we have a completely different culture at TPC.

In addition to breaking the big goal down into smaller milestones, we've managed to achieve each segment of the vision by constantly realigning to our ten-year goal and being very clear about what needs to happen next.

That task has been accomplished through the contributions of each TPC physio and their personal interactions with residents. On any seven- to eight-hour workday, a TPC physio works with approximately ten to sixteen elderly residents, and each of these consultations helps TPC grow and contributes to the team's long-term vision of two million consultations.

Each interaction that a TPC physio has with a resident helps to build a professional relationship that typically ends up being a professional friendship. We have the privilege of helping elderly folks where they live, and we get to work with them individually to help improve their quality of life. In spending all that time with the residents, their families and the staff and managers at the facilities where we work, we really get to know them.

A clear vision with measurable goals is just as powerful in attracting new recruits as it is in engaging and retaining existing team members—all of whom are essential in fulfilling that vision. Therefore, I would advise other culture-focused leaders to find a way to clearly, concisely and simply share the vision with everyone as often as possible, and do your very best to make sure your CEO and leadership team are on board with the strategy and telling stories around bringing your vision to life.

SIX WAYS TO MAKE A COMPELLING PAINTED PICTURE VISION:

1. **Make it clear**: A three-year Painted Picture vision is an inspiring, easy-to-read document.

2. **Make it specific**: Measurable goals are the easiest to manage, track and achieve.

3. **Make it possible**: Hitting goals aligns a team; missing them doesn't.

4. **Communicate progress often**: Measure, track and share progress as often as possible.

5. **Obsess over it**: Talk about your vision coming to life at least once every day.

6. **Make it fun**: The Physio Co has a basketball ring in our office with our goals painted on it!

END-OF-CHAPTER CHECKLIST

✓ Do you have a three-year Painted Picture vision of your culture's future that you refer to daily?

✓ Is your Painted Picture vision used to recruit new team members that help grow your culture?

CULTURE IS EVERYTHING
SECRET #3

EXECUTE RELENTLESSLY

CHAPTER 6

A SOLUTION TO LONG AND BORING MEETINGS: TWELVE MINUTES OF POWER

WHO LIKES LONG, BORING meetings? Not me. Who likes long meetings? No one! As you grow a business, and if you want to grow a really strong culture, then you need to have regular communication. But you need a way to stop it from being painful.

There's a solution to long, boring meetings, and that is a short, sharp, twelve-minute meeting called a huddle. The catch is that you have to do it every single day.

A daily huddle is a bit like a time-out in a basketball game: the team comes together for a short time to discuss the next move. In basketball, that means deciding who will do what and when—each player has a role to fill—and then the team leaves the huddle with an extra oomph of energy.

A daily huddle is much the same: in our huddle at TPC, which we call 'To the Point' (because, naturally, everyone has to be very 'to the point' in a twelve-minute meeting), we take a short break (twelve minutes), stand in a huddle (don't sit), share our daily priorities to ensure we are all aligned to the Painted Picture vision, raise any challenges or roadblocks and then confirm who is doing what by when (daily priorities) to focus and re-energise.

TO THE POINT

Let me explain. At about 10:03 every morning at The Physio Co, the five to seven people in our support office team get out of their chairs. They climb up half a dozen stairs and walk into the Ben Hosking Room, also known as the Huddle Room. That's where we have our short, sharp twelve-minute meeting every single day. Looking straight ahead as you walk into the Ben Hosking Room, you can see a wall full of photos of smiling members of The Physio Co family. Every member of TPC has a photo on the wall—they're the ones doing the doing, and we remind ourselves of these super-important team members helping seniors stay mobile, safe and happy every day.

Turning to your right, you can see a wall full of whiteboards. All the numbers regarding how we're going to bring our vision to life and what we need to do today, this week, this month and this year are clearly mapped out. Turning to your left, you can see a really big version of our three-year Painted Picture vision. Having the vision visible in every room of your office is a very, very, very important part of bringing your culture and your vision to life. The last wall in the Ben Hosking Room has another whiteboard—what we call the 'Where Are You Stuck Board'. The Where Are You Stuck Board is a critical part of this short, sharp daily meeting.

In our To the Point daily huddle, we have a captain who runs the meeting. That person at The Physio Co is named Jess, and it's her job to get us there on time, keep us on track and make sure we get through the agenda in twelve minutes. At 10:05 every morning, Jess gives us a big, warm, positive welcome to our daily To the Point huddle. She lets us know of any visitors coming into The Physio Co, and she makes sure we are aware of any changes happening that day in our office or team.

We then have a one-minute 'Memorable Moment'—typically a short joke, a quick game of hangman, a mini-quiz, a few facilitated deep breaths or something similar. It's fun, lighthearted and memorable to help everyone get energised.

The next thing Jess does is ask what's going on, and all of the five to seven support-team members share their top three priorities for the day—the three things they're going to do that day to help us get one step closer to bringing our Painted Picture vision to life. Even if they get distracted or interrupted, like we all do, or if the day gets derailed. Those three priorities need to be very actionable and very clear. They need to be 'start something', 'finish something', 'draft something', complete part two of something', etc—very clear actions that we can all understand.

Next on the agenda is 'Department Spotlight'. Each of us attending To the Point is head of at least one department—like finance, operations, people, recruitment and business development—so, one day per week we each get five minutes to share what's happening in our department. As the CEO, I get my five-minute spotlight on Wednesdays, where I can go into more detail about what I'm working on that week, what's important to me at the moment and how I can share my priorities with other people to bring them along so we're all part of the team. Every Department Spotlight also includes a story of how a core value has been lived.

Next up is 'Where Are You Stuck?'—possibly the most important part of the agenda. It's where we all get a chance to stick up our hand and say, 'I'm stuck here. I'm blocked. There's something I can't get done' or 'There's something The Physio Co hasn't created yet. There's a system that we need to build'. The issues raised here range from minor ('We've run out of toilet paper! Can we please get some more toilet paper as soon as possible?!') to major ('Our accounts department can't get in touch with a major client, and that client owes us $50,000. How are we going to communicate with them and how are we going to collect our money?')

Once we've raised a challenge, we write it on the Where Are You Stuck Board, along with the initials of the person responsible for solving it (who may or may not be the person who raised it) and the date that it will be solved by. We don't try to solve these challenges within the twelve minutes of To the Point; instead, we record them and then take them offline to be solved later. More often than not, the Where Are You Stuck issues are solved in conversations that happen soon after the To the Point meeting is finished.

Next we move to the very last part of the agenda, 'Today's TPCer', a one-minute update on one of our team members. There are over a hundred members of The Physio Co family, and every day we focus on one of the physiotherapists who are part of the team. We give a quick update on what that person is up to, which team they're in, which facilities or areas they visit, anything unique or interesting about the work that they've been doing recently, any holidays coming up, any study they're doing and anything of note about their professional life that they've shared with us, because as The Physio Co support team it's our job to be connected with all that team. When that TPCer calls in, we want to make sure we are up to date with what's happening in their world. That's the last part of the agenda.

Then Jess wraps us up, and within twelve minutes we've covered all those things: we've aligned our personal priorities to the future of the business, we've gotten an update on what people are working on, we've made sure we have all the systems in place or identified roadblocks, and we've stayed connected to The Physio Co family—all in a twelve-minute meeting that happens every single day at The Physio Co. That is how you can have great communication without long, boring meetings.

What I've just described is the well-drilled TPC version of a daily huddle. Although it is tailored to our business (Memorable Moment is from our core value of 'Be Memorable', and Today's TPCer is an addition we made), it's based on the three-step agenda that Verne Harnish describes in *Mastering the Rockefeller Habits*.

The Physio Co's daily huddle wasn't nearly so sharp in the early days. I personally was the To the Point captain for the first two years, and we initially only had a huddle on Mondays, Wednesdays and Fridays. At that stage, we only had a four-person support team, and having a huddle three days a week felt like enough. Interestingly, one year during December when I was on leave, the three remaining support team members decided that over the two-week Christmas/New Year period it was so quiet and so little was happening that they didn't need to have a huddle. But by about 11 a.m. on the second day, one of the guys said, 'I feel like I don't know what's going on around here. I think we need our huddle!' The other two people felt exactly the same, so they stood up and had the huddle. That very moment made us realise that we definitely needed a regular huddle and that from then on it should be daily.

Having held a regular huddle since 2009, I can confidently say that it has been one of the most valuable rituals we have created and had the discipline to stick to. Improvements in teamwork, communication, accountability, energy, growth and profits have all occurred in the years since starting a huddle.

Pulsing faster by committing to a regular meeting rhythm and almost religious discipline are some of the keys to growth.

END-OF-CHAPTER CHECKLIST

✓ Do you have an energetic daily huddle that aligns everyone to the Painted Picture vision of your culture's future?

✓ Is your culture reinforced with a short, specific story of a core value being lived at every daily huddle?

✓ Have you reverse engineered your three-year and ten-year goals to annual, monthly and weekly targets that are tracked at your daily huddle?

✓ Do you have a dedicated huddle room that visibly portrays your culture?

CHAPTER 7

A ROBUST RECRUITMENT PROCESS TO HIRE FELLOW ZEALOTS

In mid-2014, TPC expanded to start visiting elderly clients in another new state: South Australia (SA).

Our recruitment team was working as hard as they could on the important project of finding our first SA TPCers. We needed both physio team members and a team leader.

Interestingly, there was an applicant being considered for the team leader job that our recruiters needed a second opinion on. They weren't 100 percent convinced that Mike was the right fit to join our team.

As part of the team-leader recruitment process, I am involved in the second interview. In my interview with Mike, I spent lots of time asking questions and listening closely to check on the concerns of our recruiters from the earlier interviews.

After my interview, I was convinced that Mike may be our next team leader, and I was comfortable that the recruitment process keep moving. The other TPC recruiters and I had a robust chat and worked through the questions they had to resolve their earlier concerns. So, with all of us being happy and thinking Mike was a possible TPCer, we moved to next steps including an interview and reference checks.

Mike was successful in our recruitment process, he did become a TPCer and three years on he has grown into an important team member with responsibility to help us grow faster into retirement living and community care. Without a robust, multi-step and multi-person recruitment process that may never have happened.

A STRONG CULTURE NEEDS every team member aligned to the same vision and living the same values. It also needs every new recruit to 'lift the average' of the existing high standards.

That might make sense, but 'How on earth do you do it?' is a question I get asked all the time. Sometimes the best way to learn is to understand the experiences of others, so here's an overview of the approach TPC uses right now for finding great people.

Firstly, the criteria TPC uses to assess potential new hires is:

1. **Culture Fit**: An ability to *effortlessly* live The Physio Co values is our definition of culture fit. From the start of the process, we want applicants to be able to provide plenty of examples of how they live (and have lived) our core values in other parts of their life. Applicants firstly need to be able to share their experiences to us in writing, and then they need to talk about them again when we meet face-to-face.

2. **Passion for Seniors**: TPCers love to work with older people. You must have more than just a willingness to work with seniors but also an interest, a curiosity and a real passion for this type of work. We know it's not for everyone, so we want only those people who have a genuine affinity for it to join the team.

3. **Passion for The Physio Co**: We expect people to prepare and do their research when applying to join TPC. They need to understand and be aligned with our core purpose, core values and vision. Only when there's alignment between us—why we exist and what we're trying to achieve—and a new team member's personal and professional goals do we get the best fit in a new TPCer.

4. **Key Skills**: Of course, applicants must be qualified for the job they're applying for. They must also have easily contactable references from qualified professionals who are willing to vouch for the applicant's skills.

Secondly, with the criteria set, a robust and exhaustive hiring process is used that has been built from experience and is based on Brad and Geoff Smart's Topgrading approach.[6]

---

6   Brad and Geoff Smart's Topgrading approach is a process that digs deep into the personal and professional history of every potential new hire to give the best chance

Every potential new hire goes through the following seven-step selection process before a job offer is considered:

1. **Written application**: This needs to include a letter that answers the question 'Which of The Physio Co's four core values resonates with you the most and why?' (Remember to 'Be Memorable'!)

2. **Fifteen-minute phone interview**: This is essentially a brief introductory call with a few targeted questions to quickly decide if the person should continue through the process.

3. **First interview with two TPC recruiters**: This interview almost exclusively assesses culture fit. A majority of the questions are around our core values and Painted Picture vision, but there are also questions like: 'On a scale of one to ten, how lucky are you in life?' 'How would your friends describe you?' and 'Tell us about the most rewarding patient you ever worked with and why.' We want to keep applicants on their toes, ensure a memorable interview experience and be sure we are only selecting the best fit culturally. All short-listed applicants receive a copy of the Painted Picture vision when they arrive for the interview; they are given time to read the document and are then asked questions such as 'If you join TPC, what will you do to help us bring this vision to life?' The TPC recruiters that complete the first interview are required to complete a scorecard after the interview is completed. Known as the 'Post-Interview Size-Up!' this scorecard rates the applicant on: TPC-ness (values alignment), passion for seniors, communication skills, love for learning and flexibility. It

of selecting the best people.

asks the recruiters to decide why they are considering hiring this person, with questions such as 'Are we considering this person because we *really* need someone to fill this position, or is this person truly a great culture fit?' and 'Does the applicant seem to be all about him or herself or all about the job?'

4. **Skills assessment**: The skills-assessment tests around likely scenarios and can include written, verbal and/or role play. We want to ensure that the experience, reasoning and communication skills for technical concepts needed for the job are at the high standards required to become a member of the TPC team.

5. **Site visit to an aged-care home**: Applicants participate in a site visit with one or more existing TPC team members to experience the work and work environment first-hand. Occasionally, we'll do the site visit right after a phone screen. When the site visit is bumped up the list, we progress to the interview with TPC recruiters only if the applicant performs well during that facility visit. We do this because we want to make sure prospective TPCers really understand what the job is about—where he or she will be working, what it will look like, what the facility staff and TPCers are like. If an applicant has never been to an aged-care home and doesn't obviously understand what aged-care is like, then we want to ensure his or her expectations are similar to ours as early in the process as possible. The last thing we want to do is hire and train someone, then have that person be so uncomfortable with the aged-care environment that they quickly leave. The site

visit assesses for culture fit and provides the TPCer some insight into the applicant's skill set. After the site visit, the TPCer completes a scorecard on the applicant, including a recommendation for whether the applicant should continue on in the process.

6. **Second interview**[7]: This is a second interview with at least one different TPC recruiter (and it often involves the CEO) asking different questions from those asked in the first interview. The second interview is also followed by scoring of the applicant against established criteria.

7. **Three reference checks**: We check with references that TPC recruiters select from the applicant's CV, interview responses and professional history.

The reason TPC has such a robust recruitment process is twofold: We want to find out as much as we can about the potential hire as a way of beginning to build that family-like culture at the earliest stages of the relationship. We also want to share as much as we can about TPC and the existing TPC team so that the potential hire can get to know us—we want to make sure anyone who comes on board knows what he or she is getting into with this group of 'aged-care zealots'. I say that jokingly, of course, but by now I hope you see what a committed group we are when it comes to aged care.

Building a strong workplace culture is one of the most sustainable competitive advantages any business can build. This robust seven-step selection process works for The Physio Co. I hope that in learning how we select new team members, you might be better able to build, refine or improve your selection systems.

---

7   A second interview is not always required. It's most commonly included for recruitment of senior leadership positions but not for every role.

WHY 'MAYBE' MUST ALWAYS BE 'NO' FOR CULTURAL FIT

To maintain a strong culture, selection is as much about keeping the wrong people out of your team as it is about getting the right people in.

At Zappos, people who don't fit their culture are referred to as 'polluters'. I love the simplicity of this term because I've seen it first-hand at TPC too. When the wrong people join a team, they quickly start to pollute and dilute the very culture that you've worked so hard to create.

At The Physio Co, we have a firm belief that before selecting a new team member, there must be a clear 'YES' for cultural fit from existing TPCers involved in the selection process. At any point throughout the seven-step selection process, if any existing TPCer involved in the process is not 100 percent convinced that an applicant is the right person to join The Physio Co family, then that applicant is unsuccessful. A 'maybe' from anyone in the process that cannot be resolved so they feel confident in the potential TPCer joining the team is a definitive 'no'. Our culture is far too important to risk employing even one person who could damage that.

Selecting the right people is a critical task that leaders must nail. Near enough isn't good enough. Are you disciplined enough to say no to every 'maybe' that you meet?

THE REFERRAL PROGRAM

For a long time, I thought that our most likely source of referrals for new team members would be from our existing team members. I personally studied with a hundred other physiotherapists while in college, and I'd certainly refer them to a job opportunity if I thought it would work well for the physio and the employer. I'd spoken to plenty of other physios and understood that most felt the same.

So with that in mind, and with a real need to find more physios, a number of years ago we decided to communicate this need to our current team members and ask them if they would help us to find the next TPCer. We didn't get a very strong response at first, so we decided to make the idea more interesting by adding a reward.

We started by offering one day of annual leave for anyone who referred a new team member. We thought this was a great idea, but we were pretty much alone in that praise—no one offered up a referral for that reward. We upped the reward to two days and still got no real response.

Today, if a TPCer recommends someone, and that person goes through our recruitment process, joins the team and becomes a permanent member of the team, we'll give the referring TPCer one extra week of holiday time—five days of leave.

That is something that has resonated with our team, and it has been our referral reward for the last couple of years. Several of our current TPCers came to us as referrals.

REWARD YOUR ZEALOTS

As you can see from this chapter, it's not easy recruiting top talent. Even before a new employee steps through our door for the first time, we've run that individual through our recruitment process to determine if he or she can execute relentlessly. But whatever we ask an employee to give, we always give something back in return. Rewarding employees for referrals is part of what we do to give back. The logic is that if your culture asks more from your people, the culture needs to give them more in return. That brings us to the checklist's final secret: Show More Love.

END-OF-CHAPTER CHECKLIST

✓ Is your recruiting process robust enough for you to know when 'maybe' means 'no' in order to *only* hire fellow zealots?

CULTURE IS EVERYTHING
SECRET #4

SHOW MORE LOVE

CHAPTER 8

SHOW MORE LOVE

Retention, Appreciation and a Memorable First Day

WHY DON'T MY TEAM MATES work harder? I'm not asking them to work all day and all night, but while they're here, why don't they work as hard as they're capable of? Why don't they love the business like I do?

These are the questions I used to ask myself in the years before I figured out something very simple: Why *would* they? Why would anyone show more love to me, work, teammates or customers if he or she wasn't being shown any love from their boss?

We all spend a huge amount of time at work, therefore we need to find a way to enjoy it. If we're going to trade our time for someone else's money, then we may as well do it in a place where we are appreciated and loved and where we feel like we're doing something useful for others. I also reckon we need to do it in a place where we're encouraged to smile, joke and make friends with the people around us.

My original plan, when I sheepishly started working with elderly people in 2004, was to find a job that inspired me so that I'd show up and give my all every day. I dreamed that the job would also have other positive people working there who were both inspired and inspiring. I never did find that job, so I went about creating it.

The problem was that over the years as I'd progressed from working as a caring, hands-on physiotherapist for each of my clients, I hadn't progressed as well to a caring hands-on leader for each of my team members.

At a point around the time of the fifth-year struggle in 2009, it became crystal clear that if I wanted people to care more for the work they were doing and the people they were doing it with, I needed to be more obviously caring to each and every one of them. The even greater realisation was that I really did care for my team members; I loved them and was so grateful for the work they were doing, but I hadn't told them or been obvious enough in the way I'd been communicating that love. I'd become too 'busy' to show the love that I really did feel (and possibly I was again expecting everyone to read my mind).

This 'Show More Love' chapter includes a number of ways that team members can be cared for, loved and inspired to give their all.

A MEMORABLE WELCOME EXPERIENCE

Once you've found and employed a person you believe is the right culture fit, there's still plenty to do to set them up for success. (People can't read your mind, remember!)

Let's start with a question that always perplexes me: Why are parties for team members nearly always saved until the day that person leaves?! I think it's crazy that most teams only throw a party to celebrate a valued team member when that person has broken up with them and is moving on to work somewhere else.

A recruitment process is much like dating. Two people who are somewhat interested in each other make initial contact (job application); if they like each other, they schedule a date (first interview); if that date goes well, there is likely to be another date (second interview); if the dating continues to go well, they will potentially get engaged (job offer and agree to work together); and finally they might decide to get married (start working together).

In my experience, getting married means a wedding, and a wedding nearly always means a party! I don't know many people who'd choose not to celebrate their wedding and would wait until at least one person leaves the relationship to have a party. But that's what happens when we save the party until a team member leaves. It's ridiculous!

The *Culture Is Everything* process that a new hire experiences as he or she becomes a member of The Physio Co family is the example I'll use to talk you through what needs to happen next. Bear with me, I'm about to get into quite a bit of detail here, but by the end of the chapter I think you'll agree it's worth it.

At The Physio Co we are so focused on celebrating and recognising our team members that the partying starts the moment a new team member joins our family.

The very first day a team member joins us is called a 'Welcome Day'—it is a day to honour that individual. We prepare for that member. We make sure that all team members in our support office know the name of the new person joining us. The training room where he or she will be inducted into our culture is set up with his or her very favourite chocolate or treat that we've researched beforehand, and we welcome that person to the family with a hug, a high five or a handshake, and we really celebrate them from the moment of arrival.[8]

That first morning of education and induction is about sharing The Physio Co story with the new team member, going into great detail around core values, behaviours, and expectations of a new team member so that he or she understands what's expected from the start. We strive to be clear on the journey that The Physio Co is on and the behaviours that are required to be a fantastic contributor to The Physio Co story.

At lunchtime we have a welcome party in honour of the new team member(s) joining us on that given day. Members of the support team come to the party. We buy the new TPCer lunch, we have some fun, have a chat, get to know each other, talk about ourselves and of course about The Physio Co. We get to know a little about the new member's personal and professional life—what's important in his or her life, hobbies and what we might have in common. Lastly, we actually do have a little formality (like speeches at a wedding) where we raise our glasses to propose a toast that shows our excitement and appreciation of this newest TPCer having chosen to join our team. The speech often sounds something like this: 'We're rapt that you're here as a part of The Physio Co family. This party is in your honour and we're so pleased that you chose to join TPC'.

After the party on Welcome Day, the induction continues on to more job-specific training. Before the first day is over, we make sure the new team member is introduced to his or her team leader, can

---

8   I vividly remember working late into the night, or even into the early hours of the next morning, with my wife, Kimberley, as we put together the Welcome Book for the very first of these Welcome Days for two new TPCers in early 2008. Before then, our induction had been ad hoc at best. In fact, there is one long-term TPCer who clearly remembers meeting me in the car park outside of an aged-care home, and that being both her TPC interview and initial training!

access e-mail and is completely clear on their roster in order to know where he or she is working and whom they'll be spending time with in the days and weeks to come.

Perhaps a word about how we're different is best shared from one of our own. A few years ago, we had a senior physiotherapist join the family. On her celebratory Welcome Day, she turned to me and said, 'In all my years, in all the jobs that I've had, no one's ever given me permission to have fun at work before'.

That's who we are at TPC. We are a company that likes to have fun, on Welcome Day and every day. We like to make a difference, and we like to share our dreams and goals.

A RHYTHM OF CONNECTION

The new TPCer's roster and support networks are reinforced from very early on. There are in-person and phone meetings scheduled for at least once a week with the team leader or an assigned buddy (an experienced TPCer) to help answer any questions the new TPCer has and to ensure we're meeting their expectations and that they're meeting ours.

The new TPCer spends time shadowing his or her team leader or buddy to learn the TPC way until he or she is comfortable with the job and we're comfortable with the work they're doing.

In addition to having a team leader and buddy to call on, new TPCers receive two 'happiness-monitoring calls' in their first ninety days from a member of our Support Team, asking for ways we can improve their experience and to provide any additional support or training.

Four times a year, the team leader meets with each TPCer to conduct a quarterly review, what we call 'The Quarterly'. Similar to a performance review, this is a chance for the team leader and TPCer to discuss what's working and what areas need improvement.

This discussion forms the basis of a learning plan and a set of short- and long-term goals and also touches on personal goals along with other personal topics such as how things are going with the TPCer's family or any holiday plans or study opportunities.

Staying Connected

At TPC our preferred method of communication is face-to-face, because we think in-person conversations are the most effective, engaging and memorable. That's one reason we have a number of all-company events where we get people in the same room, and that's why we schedule our team leaders and our physios to spend time with each other at aged-care homes every week of the year.

Our second preferred mode of communicating is also verbal but on the phone. We think that a quick verbal conversation is so much more effective than an e-mail or social media message, but we're also a very wired organisation, with lots of options for communicating digitally: e-mail, text, Yammer, Facebook, etc.

Beyond verbal and digital communications, we also still communicate via snail mail. In addition to the anniversary and birthday cards I mentioned earlier, I send out a TPC update by regular mail to each team member's home, personally signed by me with an update on TPC's progress and any important news.

LOVE AND RETENTION

High retention of team members is one sign of a strong culture. When retention is high, confidence is high. Who wouldn't want to be a part of a buzzing culture with high retention and excited team members asking you how you'll help bring their vision to life?

Many people think that TPC, as a great place to work, would never experience an issue with high staff turnover or low retention. For the most part, that's true. But we've also had some leaner times.

In mid-2012, we had a dip in our usually high team-member retention rate. The dip wasn't life threatening for TPC, but we did lose four or five physios from our fifty-odd person team at a time when historically it is very hard to recruit new physio team members: midwinter. The result of the drop in retention included increased pressure on our existing team because of all the work we had to do with fewer people. As the weeks went by, morale got pretty low. At this point, recruiting new team members into a stressed team with low morale was close to impossible.

How did we deal with the higher-than-usual turnover of our team members? We focused on retention. We reorganised our teams, promoted more team leaders, and supported every member of our existing team more than ever. We got laser focused on the basics of caring for the personal and professional lives of each team member. We acknowledged the great work they'd been doing, added extra resources where we could and reminded everyone of the fantastic work they were doing for our frail elderly clients. In short, we showed more love.

Slowly, but very steadily, things started to change. We all started to enjoy our jobs again, retention headed back towards our traditionally high levels and we started attracting some great new physios to join the family.

Now, years on from that tough time in 2012, The Physio Co has a team that is more than twice the size and has a stronger culture and higher retention.

THE INFLUENCERS THAT DON'T (DIRECTLY) WORK WITH YOU

Showing more love is a critical and ongoing step that is mastered by teams with strong cultures. It needs to involve simple things done regularly, including genuine appreciation and thanks. It's not only limited to celebrating, and it's not only limited to the current members of your team.

The thing is, there are some really important influencers in every single team that contribute to your culture, but they're not on the payroll. These people contribute to the opinions of your team members and experience the ups and downs of life with your employees more than you or your company ever will. I'm talking about the husbands, wives, partners, kids, friends, family and house mates of your team members. Every person I know is influenced on a daily basis by the people he or she lives with. It's so important to remember that the people outside of your team but in your team members' lives are super important to the team members and therefore to you, too. They're important, and the more you include those people in the journey of your business, the greater connection you'll have with your own team members and with the business. I strongly recommend that you communicate often with your team members and your team members' families. The way you can do that is by sending mail—and I'm talking about old-fashioned mail—in the post to the employees' homes.

We have a rhythm of celebration at The Physio Co, as described in chapter 9, which includes a birthday card and an anniversary card to congratulate team members of the one-year, two-year, three-year, four-year, etc. anniversary of joining The Physio Co family. We make sure we send those cards to the home address of the team members. That card, letter of praise or inspiring all-company update you send to people's homes is much more likely to be read and appreciated by family members than any e-mail or text hidden on a device somewhere at work.

A BUDGET FOR WHEN BAD STUFF HAPPENS

A culture of celebration is important, but a culture of caring and understanding is even more important. Everyone's life has ups and downs. Sometimes things go well and sometimes they go not so well. That's a fact and a culture that understands that is important. If there's a budget that would help in acknowledging those tough times in people's lives, I suggest you have an unlimited one.[9]

---

9   This is something that I learned from Tom Peters. In his book *The Little Big Things*, Tom suggests that you have an unlimited budget for flowers, and we have the same approach at The Physio Co.

If something goes wrong in a team member's life, or in the life of someone who's important to that person, we buy a bunch of flowers, a hamper or a gift and we send it to that person's home address with a personalised note.

An example was when the wife of one of our team members, Riddick, was midterm in her pregnancy when she became unwell, and they were worried about the baby.

Riddick's wife ended up in hospital, so we sent a gift to her hospital bed saying, 'Sending lots of love from your TPC Family'. The beauty of that connection was that not only did the team member and his wife feel very cared for, but it helped them to then reconnect with The Physio Co, share with us their happiness when the baby was born, bring the baby proudly into the office and also to be grateful for the caring workplace that The Physio Co provides.

Another example of this was when a team member bought a brand-new car and was so excited about it. Then the car started to have problems. The TPCer got stuck on the side of the road when the brand-new car broke down on the way into work. A week later she had another problem with the car, and finally one day she couldn't even get to work because her car wouldn't even start.

The car problems caused her a huge amount of distress. She was so thrilled about the new car at first and then so upset. When she couldn't make it to work because of the car, we sent a bunch of flowers to her house to say, 'Hey, we know things aren't going great, but we know that they can get better from here'. That small acknowledgement of a challenge in a personal life goes a long way.

There are other ways that we do this. For example, a team member, Pete, went off and had to have an operation on an injured knee, so we sent him a hamper of books and magazines to pass the time and endure the recovery. There are many ways you can do it, but if you acknowledge that there are ups and downs in people's lives, and you have a budget to be able to send something small and personal to acknowledge it, then that caring approach will significantly help your connection with those individuals and also the connection as a team.

THANK YOU

For me, the best way to show more love and become a better, more caring leader is something very simple: saying thank you. At the end of every day to every member of the team that I am with that day, I say thank you.[10] 'Thanks for your help today', 'I really appreciate what you've done', 'Thanks for being such a great TPCer'—these short, heartfelt moments that end the conversations I have with our team members are the truth. It was, and still is, how I feel about the work that each member of our team does every day. But when I say thanks, it becomes more obvious. When you start showing more love, you often start receiving more love in return.

RANDOM ACTS OF TPCNESS

TPC team members are empowered to do the thanking! Our creator of energy and inspiration is allocated a small budget to perform 'Random Acts of TPCness' every month (and she can delegate this power to anyone and everyone).

This initiative is a great way for TPCers to thank each other and their patients and really evens things up so that all the thanking doesn't have

---

10 'Thank you' are the two most important words in business (and probably in life). I use them as often as I can. How about you?

to come down from management. TPCers really enjoy being able to thank each other.

Examples of random acts include a TPCer buying a bunch of flowers for a TPCer who had sadly lost her cat and another TPCer buying a new pair of sunglasses for an elderly resident who couldn't afford them.

The impact on the TPC culture and effectiveness of our team has increased by such a phenomenal amount since focusing on a clear, caring and structured experience for TPCers showing more love to each other.

END-OF-CHAPTER CHECKLIST

- ✓ Does every new team member get a memorable and supportive welcome on their first day?

- ✓ Does every team member get regular and personalised recognition for adding to your culture?

- ✓ Does every team member get regular and genuine appreciation from the CEO and/or senior management?

- ✓ Do you have a generous budget to show your love for team members and their families when bad stuff happens at home?

CHAPTER 9

A RHYTHM OF PARTIES AND CELEBRATIONS (AND EVEN MORE LOVE!)

DO YOU TAKE YOURSELF a bit too seriously sometimes? I know I do. If we let it, business can become all work and no play. Yes, work is an important part of our lives, but we need to find a way to enjoy it, too. Maybe encouraging and supporting a culture of celebration can help you make that happen?

Like many entrepreneurs, I'm a big fan of Richard Branson— the 'entrepreneur's entrepreneur'. One of the many things I've learnt from Richard is the importance of finding a reason to celebrate. Parties and celebrations create shared memories, and those memories can be the basis for building the strong personal relationships you need for a strong culture. At Virgin, Richard has found a way to throw a party and celebrate as often as possible, and we've embraced the same approach at TPC.

For many reasons the line 'We take the time to celebrate milestones and successes' is part of The Physio Co core value of 'Be Memorable'. One of those reasons is that I love birthdays. Even more than birthdays, I love birthday cake. In the early years of The Physio Co, when I worked full time as a hands-on physiotherapist in a heap of aged-care facilities, there were so many milestone birthdays, and I tried hard to never miss an eightieth, eighty-fifth, ninetieth, ninety-fifth or—my favourite—hundredth birthday! I'd find a way to sing happy birthday and eat cake as often as possible. Important events, big and small, happen in the lives of team members, clients, customers and suppliers every day. Acknowledging these victories and joining in the fun of a celebration that is so important to someone else will immediately strengthen the bond you share.

So today, guided by our 'Be Memorable' core value and the words 'We take the time to celebrate milestones and successes', TPC has created a culture of celebration and an annual rhythm of parties that has become super important.

We're a fairly spread-out group across Australia, but one of the ways we stay connected is through a rhythm of parties and celebrations for the TPC family as a whole. We have three all-company events throughout the year, and they are very much a celebration.

THE PARTIES

The rhythm of celebrations starts off in February each year when we have our very own birthday party. TPC was founded and first launched in February 2004, and that's when we say TPC was born. So every February we have a party to celebrate TPC's birthday. The birthday party is usually combined with another event; it might be a learning event or a professional-development day, but we make sure we have a cake, sing happy birthday and have some fun to celebrate the passing of another year in which we've helped thousands more seniors stay mobile, safe and happy. What's great about the birthday party is that it always centres on a theme. For example, our February

2015 party theme was 'Where's Wally?' (a nod to the popular 'Where's Waldo?' cartoon character in America). At that gathering, some eighty members of our team arrived wearing red-and-white striped outfits. We had some pretend spectacles and hats and canes, and we had a lot of fun dressing up as 'Wally'. Drinks and cake were served, and we sang happy birthday to TPC.

The second big day on The Physio Co's rhythm of all-company parties is in August, when we have something called TPC Swarm. It's a one-day conference—our team members come into Melbourne from all over the country and we have a full day of learning, celebrating, and recognising team members for the great work they've been doing. TPC Swarm includes one of our energetic MVP awards ceremonies, and at the end of the day we go to the bar and have a few drinks together.

The last big party of the year is The Physio Co's Christmas party. This is usually a lunchtime celebration held on the weekend. It's a fairly relaxed Christmas event, and we invite not only the TPC family but also spouses, partners and kids. Usually around 140 people come to the party, which includes fun and games, a luncheon and a gift for each member of the TPC team and everyone else in attendance.

I do my very best to personally hand out these gifts and to say hello to everyone at the party. For non-TPCers, I like to introduce myself and say something like, 'Thanks so much for being a part of the extended TPC family. It's awesome to have you here to celebrate'. Usually the gift is something small like a voucher or box of chocolates. Santa also attends this event every year to add to the fun. He hands out a gift to every child to wish them a Merry Christmas and thank them for being part of the TPC family too. They love it!

There is one formal part of the TPC Christmas party, and that's where I give a short speech to update everyone as to where we are on the TPC tally and to fill everyone in on what we're working on at The Physio Co, what's gone well during the year, what's been a challenge and where we're headed. I do this because I think it's really important that we have the buy-in and support of the families. We also announce our MVP of the Year during the reward-and-recognition program portion of our Christmas party.

It's a very special event to announce our MVP of the Year along with why they were nominated and why they are receiving the award. The person's family is nearly always in the room, and it's humbling and inspiring for the individual but also for his or her family or partner, as they know how hard the MVP has been working.

These are the three big parties at TPC, but we also have smaller events throughout the year. We encourage individual teams (groups of six to twelve TPCers in different geographical regions around Australia) to have their own rhythm and their own informal ways of celebrating milestones and successes.

For example, one team has a monthly get-together where they all go out for dinner and then do something fun like go bowling or take in a movie. That monthly catch-up is also a celebration of something special or an achievement that's happened that month, on or off the job, like a birthday, a team member buying a new house or a graduation.

REASONS TO CELEBRATE

The impact of these events is hard to measure in dollar terms but clearly palpable in terms of engagement, energy and alignment. The all-company events are not only an opportunity to celebrate, but they're also a great way for us to continue to share important messages with team members.

If for some reason one or more of our parties is missed, the energy and momentum of TPC starts to slow. We seem to pulse to this rhythm of parties, and the bigger you grow the faster you need to pulse.

Parties and celebrations don't have to be expensive, but they do need to mean something. For example, The Physio Co's very first Christmas Party was just four people going out for a meal at a local pub. It wasn't fancy, but it was very important to acknowledge, thank and celebrate with our early team members. Two of the four people at that very first party are still full-time members of The Physio Co family today!

If you want a stronger culture, start finding things to celebrate. Then throw some regular parties!

Many people think that great places to work with strong cultures are spontaneous, crazy joints where no one really knows what will happen next. In my experience, that myth is just not true. At The Physio Co, we have heaps of fun—some of it is spontaneous, but plenty of it is planned. It takes a compelling vision, consistent effort and lots of discipline to keep the excitement flowing. From Google to Zappos and every other organisation with a strong culture, robust systems to keep the culture alive are one of their obsessions.

Creating a great culture with thousands of caring moments throughout every year is our goal. But we can't forget to capture those moments.

THE CULTURE BOOK

One thing that truly sets us apart is our annual TPC Culture Book, which we release at the annual TPC birthday party in February.

We began putting the book together in 2012 as part of our ongoing cultural evolution. The book contains excerpts that speak to TPC culture in the words of our TPCers.

Late in the year, around November or December, I e-mail every member of the TPC team and ask a couple of short questions to get individual thoughts on the culture of TPC. The questions might be 'How does being a member of TPC make you feel?' 'What's unique about TPC?' or 'What is TPC's culture?' We ask different questions every year to get a variety of responses over time. For example, for the 2014 book we asked people to describe TPC in three words, and then we created 'word clouds' that we used in some very fun and interesting pictures for the book.

Every response we receive goes into the book word-for-word, whether it's positive or not. All we do is a little bit of tidying up of typos and grammatical challenges.

We take all of these responses from TPCers and collate them, and then my wife, Kimberley, dedicates most of January to designing and editing the book. The Culture Book is effectively a yearbook—a year in the life of the TPC family. In addition to the quotes from our TPCers, the book is filled with photos of events, parties and milestones that happened throughout the year at TPC. The photos are not only from all company events but also some unique moments of personal milestones, like people getting married and having babies.

Every member of the TPC family gets a printed copy of the book at the birthday party in February. In addition to distributing the printed version of the book to TPCers, we also want to share TPC's culture with the world, so we upload it as an ebook for the world to see. We also share printed copies with our clients and prospective team members. Visit tristanwhite.com.au/culturebook to see the PDF.

The TPC team members are very proud of seeing their own faces and words and names in a printed book that is shared among their peers, their colleagues and their clients. Interestingly, the first year we created the book, in 2012, one of the senior members of our team grabbed her copy and went around the room asking everyone there to initial or sign the page that her quote was on. Now that version is an even more unique, original edition. And in 2014, the cover of the Culture Book featured two young members of the team, Tina and Dean, who were so proud to be on the cover that they had a lot of fun with their 'rock star' status for a short time—they autographed their photos on the cover for anyone interested!

People outside of TPC are often intrigued as to why an organisation would share its inner workings with the outside world through an annual printed book.

First of all, it's memorable. It provides a regular and annual platform for us to share the TPC story with our existing community and to build the community beyond that as well.

Secondly, it serves a purpose of attracting people who fit our culture and our values—I really believe that like attracts like, and those people the book resonates with may be inspired to apply and hopefully to join the TPC family. There are, of course, people who see the book and don't believe themselves to be a good fit for our organisation. Again, that's fine as well because we'd much prefer that people understand what TPC is about before they join the family rather than find out the hard way that it isn't working out for either of us later on.

Thirdly, and perhaps most importantly, the Culture Book is a way for us to highlight our past achievements, to celebrate our 'Great Place to Work' awards, and to progress us towards our goal of delivering two million consultations to Australian seniors. As an internal communication tool, the Culture Book is a collection of small mentions that make a big impact. For instance, a TPCer might read a story about someone else's interaction that really touches them and lets them relate to another TPCer, gives them ideas for how they can improve their day or opens their eyes to something positive going on around them that they hadn't realised before.

EVEN MORE LOVE: FLEXIBLE WORK

Growing businesses need great people. To get the best people and keep them on your team, sometimes you need to be a bit creative. Flexible work options could be the answer you need.

You see, the days of the full-time nine-to-fivers are getting further and further behind us. Work is no longer as rigid a part of people's lives as it used to be. Sure, people still need to pay the bills, but family and more creative interests are sometimes almost as high on the list. If you're not offering flexible work options, then look out, because someone else surely will be!

Flexible work options can include the following:

- job sharing

- eight- or nine-day fortnights

- leaving early (to pick up the kids, study, train for a marathon, walk the dogs, etc.)

- extra leave without pay

- split shifts

Here are a few points to get you started in the right direction.

PROMOTE WORK-LIFE BALANCE

Parents who combine raising kids with part-time or full-time work can be some of the most competent and capable people available. In my humble opinion, raising kids is one of the most important jobs we have, and it's pretty obvious that work should fit in with family commitments. Based on the team we are building at The Physio Co, that's exactly how many others seem to be thinking, too. Some flexible options need to be available if you are committed to attracting the best people to your business.

FOCUS ON THE OUTCOMES

Now, don't stress and think this is going to cost a fortune. Flexible work arrangements can mean more productivity for your business if you get it right. By focusing on outcomes (what your business needs to make/buy/sell) rather than process ('We work from 8:30 a.m. to 5 p.m.'), you will be able to rethink how your workplace could be more flexible. Just because you've been doing things a certain way doesn't mean they should stay like that forever.

GET STAFF INPUT

Another approach you'll need to consider is to ask your team how your business could offer more flexibility. Seriously, I'll bet some people in your team have been thinking about how their work could fit better with their lives (and still get the job done). The best people understand that your business needs to make a profit. Ask them for their input, listen closely to their responses and you may just create an even better business than you ever thought possible.

There is no doubt that flexible work arrangements are here to stay. Embrace the limitless options and focus on creating a business that works for everyone.

GIVING BACK

We have always had a focus on giving back to help people who are less fortunate. Since the nature of the job that our TPC team members do every day is already a very caring type of job, we focus on giving time and funds at a local level to causes that are hopefully valuable to other members of our community.

In addition to contributing to worthy causes, we commit as a family to charity runs, hikes, bike rides, sleep outs and other events that make a difference in our lives and others.

Furthermore, for each of the aged-care homes that we visit, we have a fund available that our TPCers can request access to in order to make a small contribution to any sort of local project that's happening in the home.

For example, a couple of years ago, a TPCer named May-Ann wanted to contribute to an art group at one of the aged-care homes that she visited, so we used TPC's allocated funds for contributing to the community and purchased two paintings. May-Ann originally only had enough money for one painting, but the residents were so excited that they allowed her to purchase two with the money she had. For these elderly clients, it wasn't about the money, it was about interaction and the recognition that one of their professional staff was very keen on buying their artwork.

Those two pieces of artwork now have a place in our support office.

END-OF-CHAPTER CHECKLIST

✓ Do you have a regular rhythm of parties to celebrate the milestones of your culture and to acknowledge the personal wins of team members?

✓ Do you document your culture with an inspiring culture book?

CHAPTER 10

THE CULTURE IS EVERYTHING SYSTEM—NOW IT'S YOUR TURN!

IN MID-2016, OUR SON Roman was born. At that time, I spent four weeks at home (about a two-and-a-half-hour drive from TPC's South Melbourne support office) before and after Roman joined us on the outside. During that month, I did a total of six hours work; mostly I was at home with my wife, our two little girls and our new baby boy enjoying that special time in our lives.

I couldn't even imagine taking a full month off a decade ago when TPC was a tenth the size we are today. How is it possible that TPC achieved a reality where we'd grown so much and I was less hands-on? By now, hopefully you see that a systemised *culture* is the way to achieve the seemingly impossible.

With a strong and systemised culture, TPC can exist for weeks at a time without my fingerprints all over it. Could you spend a month away from your office? That's the beauty of the Culture Is Everything System; it allows for long-term growth without being reliant on any one person or people.

LIFE IS ABOUT OSCILLATIONS

Of course, creating a strong culture using the Culture Is Everything System will take time. There will be things that are easily implemented in your business and things that you may struggle with. That's okay. Life is about oscillations: the inevitable ups and downs. The same applies for growing a family, a business, yourself, and of course a strong culture—there will be great times and tough times. But with persistence and patience, you will get there.

Despite a systemised approach using best practices from all over the world, leading TPC to long-term success is still a struggle that I continuously work on. I make mistakes and so should you. Mistakes are fine. The way I see it, sometimes you win and sometimes you learn. That's the environment in a business with a caring culture: It's very much a learning atmosphere in which people aren't concerned about trying something new.

BE READY FOR SIGNIFICANT GROWTH

The results of using the Culture Is Everything System may outperform your every expectation—not only in the time you will save in leading your team but the speed at which you may grow.

For example, in its first five years TPC grew from an idea to a team of twenty. That was before the Culture Is Everything System was even created.

Using the Culture Is Everything Checklist, that growth sped up as TPC became a fifty person team over the next three years. Then, as we got even better at executing the Culture Is Everything System, TPC grew even faster to become a hundred-person team with services in five states of Australia—again in just three years.

A strong culture is the only way to ensure you, your company and your people are ready for significant growth over the long haul.

Our plan for the current three-year period ending at the close of 2018 is to grow from 100 to 180 team members, which will mean we've grown significantly faster again. That's the beauty of the Culture Is Everything System: it helps you speed up growth at the same time as building a stronger culture.

AN IMPORTANT REMINDER—CULTURE IS THE CEO'S RESPONSIBILITY

A strong culture is one of the only sustainable competitive advantages that a business can create. And culture, in any business, is the responsibility of the CEO. Why is culture the responsibility of the CEO? Because it's too important to delegate.

As CEO, there is an ever-existing tension between leading the management team to grow your business behind the scenes and spending time with front-line team members and clients where the real action in every business happens. At times, I've focused too much of my time building a strong leadership and support team. That has sometimes meant that I've spent more time systemizing culture in the office and less time on the road with our physio team and clients. That's been a mistake because I haven't spent enough time checking, influencing and reinforcing the Culture Is Everything System in other parts of our business.

For example, I clearly remember a time when our quarterly performance reviews were getting put off, month after month. When I looked into why, the teams explained to me they had prioritised delivering billable services over executing parts of the Culture Is Everything System.

An imbalance is a sign you need to help your team figure out how to grow culture while still growing the business. When I understood this challenge, I got involved, helped resolve the resourcing challenge and reinforced the need to prioritise the checklist **and** deliver services by asking for help and working as a team. Your team's challenge of servicing customers over balancing culture is really your challenge. That balance is what CEOs need to pay attention to.

As a life-long student of entrepreneurial and values-based businesses, I've learnt:

- From Verne Harnish, that CEOs always need to be market-facing. That is, they need to be in regular contact with their staff and clients.

- From the research of SmartCompany founder Amanda Gome, that entrepreneurial businesses often get 'stuck' in their growth cycles when they get to a certain number of team members (i.e 10, 30, 50, 100, etc). So, the CEO needs to be prepared for likely challenges and ensure the culture stays strong through periods of change and possible resistance.

- From Richard Branson, that successful entrepreneurs should always have enough time in their life to be able to dive back into challenging parts of their businesses when they're needed. That means the CEO needs to regularly monitor the culture and be ready to get involved to lead with the right combination of humility and drive.

It's important that the CEO takes complete responsibility for the culture of their business—especially when there are challenges or sticking points that will always arrive when you are focused on growth. Yes, you can delegate some of the recurring tasks on the Culture Is Everything Checklist to others, but, it is the CEO's job to make sure the system is alive and thriving. And if there are areas that aren't working, it's your job to roll up your sleeves and sort them out.

OVER TO YOU!

Now it's your turn. You have this book in your hands. You have the TPC start-up story, lessons learned and the system behind our world-class culture. You even have the *Culture Is Everything* Checklist and the Four Secrets to Creating a World Class Culture online presentation.

To achieve phenomenal growth, move away from being a manager with not enough time to complete your job and become one of the best places to work in your industry, you need to start checking off boxes. Simple as that.

Good luck and have a great day!

CULTURE
IS EVERYTHING

19 STEPS TO BUILDING A GREAT PLACE TO WORK

discover the core

1 Do you have a short & easy-to-understand core purpose? (Instead of a wishy-washy mission statement)

2 Can EVERY team member recite your core purpose?

3 Do you have 3-5 core values that EVERY team member can remember?

4 Are your core values used for a recognition & reward program that drives culture?

5 Are your core values used in every team member's quarterly review?

document the future

6 Do you have a ten-year obsession that acts as your North Star?

7 Does every team member get regular updates on progress towards your ten-year obsession?

8 Do you have a 3-year Painted Picture Vision of your culture's future that you refer to daily?

9 Is your Painted Picture Vision used to recruit new team members that help grow your culture?

execute relentlessly

10 Do you have an energetic daily huddle that aligns everyone to the Painted Picture Vision of your culture's future?

11 Is your culture reinforced with a short, specific story of a core value being lived at every daily huddle?

12 Have you reverse engineered your 3 year & 10 year goals to annual, monthly & weekly targets that are tracked at your daily huddle?

13 Do you have a robust recruiting process to know when 'maybe' means 'no' & only hire fellow zealots?

show more love

14 Does every new team member get a memorable & supportive welcome on their first day?

15 Does every team member get regular & personalized recognition for adding to your culture?

16 Does every team member get regular & genuine appreciation from the CEO and/or senior management?

17 Do you have a generous budget to show your love for team members & their families when bad stuff happens at home?

18 Do you have a regular rhythm of parties to celebrate the milestones of your culture AND to acknowledge the personal wins of team members?

19 Do you document your culture with an inspiring culture library or memory bank?

Need help executing this checklist? Visit **TRISTANWHITE.COM.AU** to learn about Culture is Everything Workshops & Coaching to help you nail it.

EPILOGUE

Now that you've read about my career journey, including thirteen years at TPC, I hope you've enjoyed the story of how I used a system and checklist to grow a physiotherapy start-up into Australia's Best Place to Work.

It's been an interesting and enjoyable ride for me, and I consider myself privileged to have found so many great people to come along with me on this journey. I'm thrilled to be looking forward to whatever lies on the road ahead, and I hope I've inspired you to realise that Culture Is Everything!

The clear picture of what TPC and the TPC family will look like in three, five or ten years is still very much a work in progress. But there's no question that it will be based around our core purpose and that we will obsess over retaining our strong culture by continuously executing and refining the Culture Is Everything System.

The TPC of the future will be closely aligned with the TPC of the past—we will continue on with the great work we've been doing, and everything we do in the future will be aligned to our core purpose of helping seniors stay mobile, safe and happy.

As of the writing of this book, our ten-year obsession (Big Hairy Audacious Goal) of delivering two million unique and memorable consultations by 31 December 2018 is still our North Star. We are putting in place the last piece of our Painted Picture vision, which of course aligns to December 2018. With our BHAG completed, we'll embark on a new long-term goal, which we'll share with the world in late 2018 or early 2019.

If you want to learn more about TPC, please take a look at the next page, visit us at thephysioco. com.au, join us on Facebook, check out my blog (tristanwhite.com.au), drop us a line via email or give us a call at the TPC support office. We'd love to hear from you!

AFTERWORD

TRUST IS THE DEFINING PRINCIPLE of great work-places—created through management's credibility, the respect with which employees feel they are treated and the extent to which employees deserve to be treated fairly. The degree of pride and levels of authentic connection and camaraderie employees feel with one another are additional essential components.

In collaboration with Fairfax Media, Great Place to Work Australia has been producing the *BRW* 50 Best Places to Work list since 2009. On our inaugural list, TPC was at number thirty-seven. At the time, TPC was a company of twenty-five employees; six years later, the company had almost quadrupled in headcount, employing just under a hundred employees. Maintaining culture and engagement through growth is one of the hardest tasks that leadership faces. Remarkably, throughout their exponential growth in headcount, TPC has not only maintained but increased their level of employee engagement, by twelve percentage points. In 2014, TPC achieved the number-one ranking on our list of best employers with under a hundred employees. It came as no surprise to us at Great Place to Work. For years we had been monitoring the evolution of this unique company.

CORE PURPOSE:
The Physio Co exists to help seniors stay
mobile, safe and happy.

CORE VALUES:
Respect Everyone.
Be Memorable.
Find a Better Way.
Think Big, Act Small.

Core values underpin everything TPC does. From recruitment and selection to communicating business updates, performance reviews and of course reward and recognition, the core values of Respect Everyone, Be Memorable, Find a Better Way, and Think Big, Act Small essentially align the organisation. Alignment is imperative in sustaining great workplaces, as it assists in each and every employee's understanding of how they play a vital part in helping TPC to help seniors stay mobile, safe and happy! After all, when we speak to employees at great workplaces and ask them what is so great about working at their company, the answer isn't game consoles and limitless supply of candy but rather that they believe in what the company wants to achieve and that they want to be part of that.

One of the employees at TPC summed it up perfectly: 'TPC feels more like a family unit than just a job. Milestones and achievements are celebrated, whether work related or personal. The management staff are some of the loveliest and most genuine people I have ever worked with. I am proud to be part of such a dynamic and positive team!'

Great Place to Work is a mission-driven organisation, and our mission is to help build a better society by helping companies transform their workplaces. Any company can be a great workplace, and every leadership team has the power to make it happen. It begins with an investment in building trust throughout your organisation. The return will be a more vibrant enterprise, more innovative products and more satisfying relationships. Employees who trust their managers give their best work, and their extra effort goes right to the company's bottom line. Managers who trust their employees allow innovative ideas to bubble up from all levels of the company. Employees who trust each other report a sense of camaraderie and even the feeling of being part of a family. Together they deliver far more than the sum of their individual efforts.

On our journey to transform workplaces, we celebrate great workplaces by publishing more than a hundred 'Best Workplaces' studies in over fifty countries. It is indeed gratifying to see our clients not only do well but to share their stories of success with pride. I am sure anyone who takes the time to read this book will be not only entertained but also educated and rewarded.

—**ZRINKA LOVRENCIC**, managing director, Great Place to Work Australia

ABOUT THE PHYSIO CO (TPC)

TPC helps seniors stay mobile, safe and happy. Healthcare for Australian seniors is our thing.

TPC was born in 2004, sparked by passion to use physiotherapy to improve the lives of senior Australians. Founder Tristan White discovered hundreds of thousands of Australian seniors needed better physiotherapy services. He also identified that there were many health professionals not feeling challenged or appreciated in their jobs. TPC was born to fill a niche, provide a great service, and bring together a team of talented and caring health professionals.

Since 2004, TPC has grown from a one-person operation to the large team that exists today. TPC now visits thousands of residents every week. Growth at this rate is not possible without great attention to detail, outstanding customer service and ongoing quality assurance programs. The care, compassion, expertise and quality of our services results in TPC as the best health professionals in aged care and the obvious choice for client-focused providers.

TPC's service makes a positive impact on the lives of senior and elderly clients every day: Simple things can make a huge impact, like prescribing a new walking aid or implementing a fun and easy-to-follow exercise program. These results make a real difference to someone who has been frustrated and restricted in their independence.

TPC has repeatedly been recognised as one of Australia's 'Best Places to Work'. Every year, from 2009 through 2016, TPC was very fortunate to be a winner and finalist in a number of awards. The awards are a great reminder to everyone at TPC that we are making a difference. We share the good news of these awards with the entire team and invite some members of our physio team to attend the award ceremonies with the leadership team, and we have a party! Some of our awards have included:

- Ranked No. 37 in 2009, No. 19 in 2010, No. 12 in 2011, No. 8 in 2012, No. 5 in 2013, No.1 in 2014 and No. 2 in 2015 of Australia's 'Best Places to Work'.

- In 2014, voted No. 1 of 'Best Places to Work' in the Under 100 Employees category.

- Listed on *BRW's* 'Fast 100' in 2011 as one on Australia's 'Fastest Growing SMEs' (small and medium enterprises).

- Ranked in Smartcompany.com.au's 'Smart 50' list of fast-growing SMEs in 2009 and 2010.

- Tristan was ranked in Smartcompany.com.au's 'Hot 30 Under 30' of Australian entrepreneurs in 2009 and 2010.

- Tristan was a finalist in Australian Anthill's '30 Under 30'.

- TPC was a finalist in *My Business* magazine's awards 'Best Small Business' and 'Best Young Gun in Small Business'.

- Finalist in the HR Champion Awards.

- Winner of an Australian Achiever Award for excellent customer service

Read more about TPC and the founder's insights on building a magnetic company culture at: tristanwhite.com.au.

ABOUT THE AUTHOR

Tristan White is married to Kimberley and is dad to Alexandra, Harriet and Roman. He's a qualified physiotherapist and is best known as the founder and CEO of The Physio Co (TPC).

TPC is a healthcare business that exists to help seniors stay mobile, safe and happy. Allied health services for Australian seniors at aged-care facilities, retirement villages and wherever senior clients call home is what TPC does.

In 2014, The Physio Co was named No. 1 on the annual *BRW* list of Australia's 50 Best Places to Work. TPC has been ranked one of Australia's Top 50 Places to Work for eight consecutive years in its thirteen-year history. In 2015 and 2016, along with being one of Australia's best, TPC was also ranked as one of Asia's Best Workplaces.

Tristan's passion is building TPC to be a thriving business with a strong and caring culture. The simple approach of creating and sticking to a simple set of rituals along with being honest, treating people with the respect they deserve and doing it all with a smile is working for Tristan and the TPC team.

TPC's team delivers hundreds of thousands of consultations to Australian seniors each year and is on track to achieve their audacious ten-year goal of two million unique and memorable consultations by the end of 2018.

Tristan loves to share what he's learnt on his entrepreneurial journey. His *Culture Is Everything* blog, over at tristanwhite.com.au, was listed by SmartCompany as one of Australia's 20 Best Business Blogs in 2011, 2013 and 2014. Tristan is regularly a keynote speaker at conferences where he shares his engaging presentations including 'The Four Secrets to Building a World Class Culture'.

To invite Tristan to speak at your next company event or conference, contact Tristan at
www.tristanwhite.com.au

CPSIA information can be obtained
at www.ICGtesting.com
Printed in the USA
BVHW061926021219
565425BV00015B/813/P